BRITTANY PETTIBONE

What Makes Us

Girls

AND WHY IT'S ALL WORTH IT

REASON BOOKS
INTERNATIONAL

For all the girls who love me, even when I don't deserve it. For my grandmother, Yolanda. For my mother, Sabrina. For my twin, Nicole. For my sisters, Natasha, Isabella and Hannah. For my friends: Juliette, Lauren, Rebecca, Melissa, Annika and Ariane. For my cousins: Anne Marie, Mary and Brisa.

Contents

About the Author

Brittany Pettibone, born in 1992 in California, is a writer and conservative political activist. Her passion for politics compelled her to enter the political scene in 2016. Since then, she has produced numerous videos, from interviewing notable right-wing figures to reporting on-the-ground across America and Europe. A long-time student of the writing craft, Brittany is the co-author of *Hatred Day*, an award-winning science-fiction and fantasy novel. *What Makes Us Girls* is her first non-fiction book. Currently, she lives in Idaho, but will relocate to Austria when she marries her fiancé in 2019.

Author's Note

There are many topics I initially wanted to explore in this book such as female friendships, equality, femininity versus masculinity, the struggles of modern dating, professional careers, marriage and children, and so on. But after writing the first chapter, I came to understand that these topics can't be adequately explored without first exploring one of the major problems that all girls, myself included, struggle with: *self-worth*. So, I've decided to dedicate the entire book to this topic.

While I will include references to all the other topics listed, I will wait to explore them fully in another book. That said, please be aware that this book is not intended to be an argument packed with facts and statistics; it's largely anecdotal, using advice and stories from my own life experience and the life experiences of girls I know as a way to be encouraging. Lastly, most of the stories in this book are true, but I have changed names, relations, dates and even genders for the purpose of protecting privacy.

1

"We know what we are, but know not what we may be."

—William Shakespeare

Dear Girls...

I didn't want to write this book. In fact, the last thing in the world I ever thought I'd be doing was writing such a book.

During my teenage years, I had very few female friends. I believed myself to have a mind more similar to the boys, and as a result, convinced myself that I would never be able to connect with girls. Ridiculous, I know. It goes without saying that this was a flawed state of mind, but it was born out of a desire to be regarded as "one of the guys," or as somehow more unique and special than other girls.

While it's true that some girls may understand or even appreciate the male mind better than others, as a whole, there is no comparison. Boys and girls are worlds apart, both mentally and physically; it was only until after I accepted this reality that I was able to see girls for the wonders that they are, or that they have the potential to be. I started to develop female friendships—not the superficial kind where girls meetup simply to gossip, but the sincere kind. The kind where competition is innocent and healthy, and where girls act for one another as confidants, advisors, supporters and companions.

Considering all the female friendships I have made, and all the girls I have come to love, is what convinced me to sit down and write this book. Not because I want to write it, but because I must write it. My intention isn't to prove nor is it to judge. My intention is simply to encourage. Perhaps you could describe this book as a love letter to all the girls I know and do not know who are experiencing the struggles of womanhood which are commonly felt but rarely discussed.

Self-Worth: The Ultimate Struggle

Do you love yourself?

If now, or at any point in your past, you would've answered "no" to this question, then you and I have something in common.

During my teenage years, and even at certain periods during my early twenties, I also would've answered "no." Like many other girls, I was battling an extreme lack of self-worth that blossomed within me like a bouquet of razors. Few of my relationships—both friendships and romances—were long-lasting, and even worse, few were sincere. But how could my relationships have been long-lasting and sincere? A person cannot give what they do not have. And since I didn't love myself, I had no love to give to others. Of course, this doesn't mean I never had the desire. I often did wish to give love, but whenever I tried, it was the equivalent of offering my bouquet of razors. Every attempt ended in a wound.

Lack of self-worth can stem from many things. Among the most common are: negative comparison, rejection, bullying, inauthenticity, purposelessness, betrayal and guilt. Obviously, any number of other issues can activate a lack of self-worth, but since the issues listed above are ones that I, and many other girls I know, have personally experienced, I will only touch upon them.

Before I begin, though, I think it's important to clarify that experiencing periods in our lives when we struggle to love ourselves is perfectly normal. Facing a lack of self-worth doesn't make us outcasts; on the contrary, it probably makes us more relatable. At one point or another, almost every girl in the entire world—no matter our age or the country we are from—will have to fight the same battle. Some of us will win and some of us will lose. But those of us who win will do so for two reasons: because we are able to see the battle for what it is, and even more importantly, because we have the right weapons to fight it.

2

"Comparison is the death of joy."

—Mark Twain

When You Think You're Not Good Enough

When I was younger, I used to paint from life—portraits mostly. Oftentimes, painting proved frustrating because no matter how long and carefully I worked, I could never precisely capture the likeness of my model. All of my finished paintings seemed lacking in comparison. Over time, I learned that "precise replication" should never be one's goal—not in art or in any other creative endeavor. Artists should strive to bring their own personal touch to their craft. Only in doing so can they provide a unique and personal vision of the world. As you may have guessed, this oppressive comparison didn't improve my painting. Quite the opposite, it hindered my progress.

Inadequacy, or the feeling of not being good enough, generally originates when we negatively compare ourselves to others, or worse, when we hear others negatively compare us.

Comparing ourselves to others is oftentimes unavoidable. One reason for this is because comparison is a natural means of measurement; it is a method by which we come to realize the quantity or value or nature of a thing. But problems arise when this comparison is either inaccurate or just plain false.

At one point or another, we have all compared ourselves to siblings, to friends or even to strangers, and most likely concluded that this or that person is better than us in some way. Perhaps we believe they are more intelligent. More humorous. More charismatic. More beautiful. More successful. In drawing such harsh and critical conclusions about ourselves, there is only one outcome: inner discontent.

The discontent might start small, in the form of harmless insecurities, but if we don't immediately make an effort to master these insecurities, eventually they will grow. They will become more and more difficult to control with each passing day, until eventually, we surrender the dominant role to our insecurities. We might even start walking down the dark and lonely road of self-hatred.

For the past two years, I've been a political YouTuber. Due to the fact that I recently got engaged, I've made the decision to pull a bit back from YouTube; I want to focus primarily on becoming a wife and a mother, and to dedicate my free time to writing books. But back when I was immersed in the vast network of political commentators, activists and journalists, I often struggled with self-comparison. Most of my fellow political YouTubers made more effective and informative videos than me. Their videos were better quality, and they also got more views. On top of this, most of them were far more intelligent and articulate. For a time, the reality that I would never be as good as them was difficult to accept. I pushed myself to absurd limits, forgoing my physical and mental health in the process. I worked so hard that I rarely slept; as the months wore on, my appearance turned hollow and sunken. I lost an unhealthy amount of weight because I didn't give myself sufficient breaks to eat. Worst of all, I had no time to spend with my family and friends, and my relationships suffered as a result.

Obviously, I wasn't happy. The only moments I felt a glimmer of satisfaction were when I made a great video that hundreds of thousands of people found useful, but this satisfaction faded after a day or so. And it would completely die the moment I posted another video that wasn't received well. It was a vicious cycle, like always drinking from a cup that was half-empty.

I'm sure most of you can already identify the problem with my mindset here because let's face it: at times, the most obvious solutions to problems can be the most difficult for us to recognize. Had I simply accepted from the beginning that I would never be as good as the other political YouTubers, had I simply been content with trying my best, I would've saved myself and those closest to me a lot of pain.

There is a common structure step in every good book called "the attack by ally," when the allies of the main character notice something that the main character is doing wrong and point it out—not to judge or criticize, but because they care about the main character and want to help. In a way, this is exactly what happened to me. My mother, who had all the while been keeping a close eye on me, eventually decided that enough was enough. She told me, in a loving way of course, that I'd stopped treating myself and others as well as I once did. She told me that my YouTube content wasn't as good as it had been in the beginning because it was less from the heart. She even told me I looked physically unhealthy, that I'd lost my spark.

I'll admit that I didn't react well initially. My transition was long and difficult. What helped was telling myself that even if my contributions were only shadows in comparison to what my fellow political YouTubers were contributing, at least I was doing something. I was giving all that I could to the best of my ability. Something else that helped was realizing that I should never have treated my fellow political YouTubers as competitors in the first place. At the end of the day, we were all a team.

Should we ever allow our insecurities to take control, as I did, they will be a source of constant pain. The natural way to ease such pain is to push ourselves beyond our limits, or even to seek validation from others, which might pressure or persuade us to make choices that go against our principles—things we would never normally do if we were in a healthy state of mind. Moreover, what happens if we don't receive the validation we're so desperately seeking, or worse, if we get the opposite? It destroys us.

Another danger of allowing our insecurities to take control is that, in some cases, they can convince us to give up on ourselves. Every task we attempt will be tortured by an inner voice telling us that we're inadequate, that we'll never be as good as those we've been comparing ourselves to. Our sense of motivation will become paralyzed and collapse. We may even stop trying altogether. And if we don't try, we will never progress. We will never achieve the remarkable things that we might've achieved had we learned to master our insecurities.

There have been plenty of times when I felt that I'd reached my limit, that I was incapable of fighting anymore. I sought refuge in places where the world couldn't see or judge me. But the one thing I could never succeed in shutting out was the knowledge that if I gave up on myself, I was finished. Nobody would be able to save me. People can help us, yes, but only to an extent. And before others can help us, we have to help ourselves. Of course, it's normal and understandable to spend a few days trying to rebuild ourselves every now and again, but eventually, we have to stand back up.

When it comes to mastering feelings of inadequacy, I've often found it helpful to consider the fact that nearly every meaningful achievement requires work: developing a skill, raising a family, making a marriage work, having a professional career. All are difficult roads to meaningful destinations.

Each human being has unique qualities, even if these qualities are small. It's why we use the term "irreplaceable." Because the person who we consider irreplaceable has qualities that nobody could ever perfectly replicate.

What are your own unique qualities? What qualities do you have that the person you've been comparing yourself to doesn't have? Perhaps you have special physical attributes or a method of treating people that makes them feel appreciated in a way that no one else can.

Also, what are your strong suits? Perhaps you're not too attractive, but you're intelligent and caring. Or vice versa: Perhaps you have the beauty, but not the brains or the kindness.

For every single one of us, unique qualities and strong suits are the foundation upon which we must build. But it's best if we do so slowly. Trying to do too much too fast will almost always result in our becoming overwhelmed and perhaps even quitting. Instead, we must take it one day at a time, one step at a time. Our most useful ally along the way will always be focus. If we're able to keep a strong focus, we'll be less inclined to continue comparing ourselves to others, for we will only have a mind for the goals that lie ahead.

We will also have much more time, energy and motivation to complete these goals.

When Others Think You're Not Good Enough

If you thought to yourself, *that girl is smarter than me*, or if somebody else said to you, "that girl is smarter than you," which remark would hurt you more? Most girls, myself included, would choose the second remark. The reason for this is because the comparison is not a personal conclusion, one that can be overcome through hard work or validation. It's an external perspective, oftentimes irreversible, and completely outside our control.

During my childhood, people often negatively compared me to my sisters. I was told my sisters were more beautiful than me, that they had a better sense of style, and that they had more talent when it came to singing, drawing and writing, and so on. When I joined political YouTube, the comparisons kicked into overdrive. Thousands of people were regularly commenting on my videos, and among these comments, negative comparisons always popped up. *Your twin sister is much more beautiful and feminine than you*, some would write. Others compared me to fellow female political YouTubers, saying that they were prettier and more intelligent.

Obviously, it's natural for such comparisons to hurt. But there is a route of combat, and it starts with examining the person who made the hurtful comparison. Do we know the person? Or are they just some random stranger who we've never met? If this is the case, it's natural to feel hurt, but ultimately, it would be silly to allow a stranger's opinion to affect our overall view of ourselves. The only opinions that should carry weight are the opinions of those we love, look up to and respect.

So, if at any point, someone who we love, look up to and respect makes a negative comparison of us, the feeling of inadequacy is completely understandable.

Of all the times I've been compared to other girls, the situation I recall hurting me the most was when a couple of male friends compared me to another girl. Of course, I had no intimate or familial attachment to the young men—we were simply political acquaintances—but the comparison still hurt. We were all packed into the car, heading home from a political protest which, at several points, had escalated into violence.

"Wow, Anna's amazing," the driver, a young man named Victor, commented. "Seriously, she's like the sweetest girl ever."

"Who's Anna?" I asked, only half-paying attention. Sitting in the passenger seat, my head slouched against the window, I was fighting off sleep. Odors of sweat and pepper spray saturated my clothing. My energy was depleted, far past my point of tolerance, and I wanted nothing more than to collapse into my bed. The back-to-back protests, rallies and speeches were beginning to take a toll. I questioned whether I was cut out for political activism, mainly because I often felt too weak to go on. My sole motivation for persevering stemmed from an ardent belief in our cause. I couldn't ignore the dire state of the West, no matter how much I wanted to, no matter how high the personal cost: my life ambitions, my security and privacy, my livelihood, my reputation, and more.

The second young man, Andrew, who was sitting in the back seat, answered, "How do you not remember Anna, Britt? She made us all dinner."

"Oh—of course. Sorry, I forgot."

I smiled sheepishly, feeling that I'd been rude. I'd met over a hundred people that day, and as a result, didn't remember most names. Eventually, an image of Anna returned to my mind: layered brown hair, a caring smile and a slender frame wrapped in a blue trench coat that was frayed at the wrists. I recalled having spoken to her for a few minutes, recalling specifically that my impression of her had been nothing short of positive.

"It was great of her to cook for us," Victor went on. "She even made us sandwiches for the drive home." He motioned to three neatly-wrapped sandwiches in the back seat.

Andrew opened one of the sandwiches and took a bite. "What girl still cooks these days?" he marveled. "If Anna didn't already have a guy, I'd call her."

"Lots of girls can cook." I laughed. "I'm not so bad."

"Hey, it's okay, Britt," Victor said. "Nobody in the movement expects that of you. We know you're not that kind of girl."

I hesitated. "Not what kind of girl?"

"You know…the maternal, caring type."

I stopped laughing as a sharp pang struck my chest.

Both Victor and Andrew noted my reaction and their shoulders stiffened, as if realizing they'd said something hurtful.

"We don't mean anything bad by it," Andrew assured. "We just meant that you're sort of different."

"You might not be as maternal as Anna," Victor added, "but Anna's not political and she could never do what you do. Most girls couldn't."

I smiled and shrugged off the conversation, passing the remainder of the trip in silence. I wasn't comforted by their words, mainly because they were wrong. I couldcook. I'd learned from one of the best cooks in the world: my mother. The reason I hadn't helped Anna make dinner was because, after spending the entire day in a riot, I was tired and distracted. Not to mention, my friends hadn't known me long. We'd never been in a situation where I could cook for them. Plus, I would have preferred to be in the kitchen cooking rather than risking my life to give a speech or film a YouTube video.

Although the young men's comparison struck a nerve in my feminine pride, for as long as I knew them, they never compared me again—at least not to my face. In this respect, communicating to our friends and loved ones how we feel is imperative. Without communication, the channel to understanding the world around us is cut. We might even end up developing a false sense of how our loved ones perceive us, which could destroy our relationships irreparably.

On the other hand, if the negative comparison was intentional and the person, even though they love us, made the comparison deliberately to hurt us because they were angry, we simply have to come to terms with the fact that people say harsh words out of anger all the time—and more often than not, they don't truly mean what they're saying in regards to insulting us. Many of us likely already understand this because we're guilty of using harsh words in moments of anger ourselves. It might take some time, but if the person loves us, eventually they'll apologize.

When You Think Others Are Not Good Enough

Growing up, my parents had house rules which they expected all of the children to follow. Naturally, being a bit of a rebel during my early teens, I often broke these rules. I remember using the negative comparison method on mother as a means to get my way. When, for good reason, she wouldn't allow me to do some activity or attend some concert or party, I'd tell her: "Why can't you just be like other mothers? Why do you have to be so strict?" Looking back, this harsh comparison must have hurt my mother, especially because her rules came from a place of love, from a desire to protect. She had my best interest in mind. And me, well...I just wanted my way.

Every girl understands the pain of being compared to others. We understand the damage it causes to our sense of self-worth because we've experienced it, which is why it's also important to ask ourselves if we've ever turned the tables and been the ones who made comparisons. If so, we are guilty of inflicting the same sense of inadequacy that we've felt onto others.

I once knew a family with two girls: Emma and Adriana. Emma was married to the type of man that many girls hope to meet—protective, loyal, hard-working, ambitious, generous, humorous and great with children. Adriana, who was unmarried, was constantly fixating upon Emma's relationship, telling herself that she wouldn't settle for or be content with a young man who didn't have all the qualities that Emma's husband had. Adriana's relationships suffered as a result; they always ended in breakups. Perhaps her relationships would've ended in breakups either way, but perhaps one might've worked out if she had simply stopped comparing her boyfriends to Emma's husband, trying to discern if they had all the qualities that she desired and criticizing them if they did not.

Few things damage a young man's confidence in himself as much as being compared to other young men, especially if the person comparing him is the girl he loves. The reason for this is that every man wants to be admired. If we are constantly criticizing him for what he isn't instead of admiring him for what he is, he might lose the motivation to improve. He might grow distant and start to resent us. He might even fall out of love with us.

While it's necessary to have standards, it's also necessary to be realistic. And the reality is that *all* human beings are imperfect. If we can't leave room for other people's imperfections, how can we expect them to leave room for ours? It would be unfair to have a fifty-page checklist that a girl must meet before we're friends with her, or that a young man must meet before we date him.

Of course, there are fundamentals—such as complimentary life goals and similar religious beliefs—that we might require in friend or boyfriend, but when it comes to the details, we must accept their imperfections and appreciate them for all the good qualities that they do have. In doing so, our friend or boyfriend might even end up developing the extra good qualities that we want.

No one is perfect. Despite what Adriana believed, Emma's husband wasn't perfect, even if he appeared so from the outside. Every friendship, every romance has its trials and struggles. The biggest difference between successful and unsuccessful relationships—no matter if the relationship involves family, friends or romance—is how we deal with the trials and struggles.

When You Think Others Are Good Enough
(And It Makes You Better)

The reason I have specifically used the term "negative comparison" in this chapter is because I wanted to make it clear that not all comparison is destructive. In fact, certain types of comparison are healthy. Perhaps you know or have seen from afar someone who you greatly admire. You look up to this person as a role model and have a desire to adopt their good qualities. Your reaction isn't jealousy, inadequacy or despair, but a strong motivation to become better. In this case, comparison can be a path to personal improvement and even success. It should never be discouraged.

At the end of the day, none of us gain by desiring, but by doing. If we direct our time, energy and motivation towards developing our unique qualities and strong suits, we will never remain stagnant or regress. We will always be moving ahead. Of course, it's inevitable that all of us will stumble a bit along the way. But sometimes it helps to remember that we're not alone. Of the three and a half billion girls who currently exist in this world, the vast majority of them will, at one point or another, struggle with the exact same feelings of doubt, frustration and inadequacy that we do.

3

"There is no doubt; even a rejection can be the shadow
of a caress."

—José Ortega y Gasset

Taking the Bitter Pill

Not a single girl I know has avoided rejection. All of them, even
the kindest, prettiest and most talented girls, have been forced to
taste this bitter pill. Sometimes, I'm shocked to discover that they
have experienced rejection, for they seem perfect—or at the very
least, they seem worlds above me. I used to deny the possibility
that there was a good reason for their rejection, and believed that
the fault must lie with the company that didn't hire them or with
the person who rejected them. But I can see now that, at least in
some cases, I was wrong. The reality is that we're not always going
to be wanted in return by who and what we want. It's not to say

that we can never develop the necessary skills or attributes to overcome rejection and become successful, it's just that we're not always going to be in a position to get the things we want exactly when we want them.

I've been rejected more times than I can count. I'm embarrassed to admit that my first reaction to rejection was something along the lines of, "Well, I don't want your acceptance anyway."

This reaction was obviously false, and I didn't truly mean it, but it was a way to compensate for the feelings of inadequacy that followed, which culminated in a desire to retreat into myself, into a shell of safeness and self-pity where I could comfort my ego. Of course, whenever we break down and allow ourselves to act in such a manner, it becomes all the more difficult for us to revive our motivation.

Like many girls, I struggle with pride. But being prideful doesn't make us bad girls; it just makes us flawed. The largest danger of pride in regards to rejection is when we allow pride to blind us to the *cause* of our rejection. For example, we might aspire after a certain job, but lack the necessary qualifications. Or perhaps we might want to date a certain young man, but lack the qualities he desires in a girlfriend. If we allow ourselves to become blinded by pride, the result is a failure to see our own shortcomings. And if we fail to see our own shortcomings, how can we improve?

I've received a lot of good advice concerning dealing with

rejection over the course of my life, but two pieces stand out above the rest.

1st Piece of Advice:
Sometimes the Signs Say Go Forward

View rejection as an opportunity to improve—like another rung on the ladder to climb, a challenge, that, once overcome, makes us stronger. If we can view rejection in this way, then we will always move forward.

Depending on the situation, we might need to improve our character, our intellect, our physical appearance or even our spiritual side. While it can be difficult, it would actually be worse for us in the long run if we achieved everything we wanted on our first attempt. Imagine being rewarded with a trophy for every competition you participated in, regardless of having won or lost. Imagine being freely given every opportunity you ever strived for, not because you earned the opportunity, but simply because you desired it. Imagine achieving all the success you ever dreamed of on a whim.

Sounds tempting, right?

The problem with instant gratification is that human beings require conflict in order to grow. Without struggle, there is no satisfaction in victory. Without working hard for success, how can we feel that we've *earned* the reward? Accomplishment achieved through work and sacrifice is vital to deep and lasting appreciation. It is also vital to personal growth. When a girl views all of her actions as "perfect," she does not have motivation to improve any aspect of herself or her life. She becomes content with stagnancy. With mediocracy. Not to mention, if there ever were to come a point in her life when she is rejected, she wouldn't know how to handle it. She would despair.

Think about all the successful girls you know. At times, it might seem like they have it all. High-powered careers. Charm. Talent. Beauty. Wealth. I can assure you that the majority of these girls walked a road of rejection before arriving at this point. Beneath the glitz and the glamour lies a memory vault of struggle that only they are privy to. In fact, it was this very struggle which eventually led them to success. The rejection they suffered might have been big or it might have been small. The difference is that, in the face of conflict, these girls didn't quit.

I think the most honest way to view success is as a series of rejections, without which a person never would've been able to reach the goal they strove for. Regard each rejection as a step, and if you're able to overcome all the steps, eventually you'll reach the top rung of the ladder.

2nd Piece of Advice:
Sometimes the Signs Say Make a Turn

Consider rejection as a redirection to alternative opportunities. Imagine life as a series of paths marked with sign posts, but sometimes the signs appear in a vague form, not quite distinguishable as signs. For example, say you're walking a path that abruptly ends with a wall. Depending on the situation, you might be meant to regard the wall not as an obstacle, but as a cue pointing you in an alternative direction.

From the age of fifteen, my life dream was to be a science-fiction and fantasy writer. Being ambitious, I aspired to be more than an average writer, one whose books spoke to people on a level deeper than entertainment. I wanted to be able to write every day, to sit in silent unification with my stories, making a full-time career out of my craft. Nine years of working towards this dream passed, and in those nine years, I received over two-hundred rejection letters from literary agents. Each rejection letter felt like a new mountain I had to climb. Of course, some of the rejections hurt more than others—for example, when I was close to success. Normally, a writer is required to submit five or ten pages to a literary agent; the agent reads the submission, and if they enjoy it, they will request the writer's full manuscript. Depending on what the agent thinks of the full manuscript, they will either make an offer to represent the writer or reject them.

Whenever a literary agent requested my full manuscript, I wasn't able to sleep for days. I would pace around my house with a strange combination of nervousness and excitement, hopeful that every new email I received was the one I was waiting for. During these times, self-doubt crept in, corroding the calm demeanor I tried so hard to uphold. I would repeatedly think things like: *Maybe the agent didn't receive my work. Maybe my manuscript email was lost. Maybe the agent hates my work and just tossed it out.*

Finally, the long-expected email arrived, but not with the decision I had hoped for.

These rejections were devastating. They often made me question whether I was even any good. Fortunately, in difficult times I had support from my loved ones, who saw the potential in me when I couldn't see it in myself. At my lowest points, it was solely due to this encouragement that I overcame the temptation to give up and continued pursuing my goals.

In hindsight, I'm thankful for each and every rejection I received because they motivated me to improve my writing craft. Had my stories been accepted and published upon first submission, I can honestly say it would have been a disaster—especially in regards to my first novel. Like most amateur writers, back then I thought my first novel was a masterpiece. Let's just say that I'm thankful that this manuscript never made it out into the world.

Undoubtedly, the most important reason I'm thankful that my

stories were never published in the mainstream industry is that, had I been accepted by a traditional publishing house and joined the ranks of successful authors, I likely never would've joined political YouTube. Yes, I might've had a desire to become politically active, but I wouldn't have had the opportunity to do so. I would've been too bogged down and consumed with writing more books, meeting deadlines, participating in book tours and attending author-related events.

Even more importantly, I never would've met my fiancé, for we met due to the fact that we're both political activists. No life in this world, no matter the level of success it offered, could ever even remotely compare to a life with him.

Hope isn't always easy to find. I admit that I've had days so burdened by hopelessness that I was unable to see a brighter future. I truly wanted to give up. On the other hand, I've also had hopeful days, brightened by the mysterious feeling that I was meant to end up with a certain person or in a certain place. Perhaps you've experienced this feeling, too. Whether you believe in God or in some kind of destiny, it's possible that all those rejections were sent to guide you there.

Dispensing the Bitter Pill

On the day when everything should have gone right, everything went wrong. Thomas was late. Snow crunched under his shoes as he sprinted into the metro station, a briefcase in one hand and his dry cleaning in the other. He elbowed his way down the crowded escalator, his swinging arms knocking a shopping bag from someone's grasp.

"Sorry," he said, holding out his hands in apology.

"Watch where you're going."

Turning, he sprinted through the station towards platform twelve. Just as he cleared the last stair on the platform, he bit off a curse. The train was leaving, its gears squealing as it glided over the magnetized tracks. He slowed to a jog, then to a walk, his stomach sinking with every step. The train sped away, its taillights winking in the dark tunnel.

"Not tonight," he said in frustration. "Any night but tonight."

An elderly woman, who was sitting on a nearby bench reading the latest issue of the *New York Post*, smiled at him through thick-rimmed glasses.

"Everyone misses a couple of trains a year," she said. "Sometimes it's a good thing, sometimes it's not. The question is: are you going to be late for something important?"

"Yes."

"Mmm…" She gave him a glance-over, her dark eyes inspecting his outfit: awhite button-down shirt under a navy cardigan, with brown dress shoes scuffed from wear."A well-dressed guy like you doesn't own a car?" she inquired.

"I don't drive."

"I see. Where are you headed?" she asked.

"Midtown."

"Next train is in twenty minutes."

Thomas consulted the train info boards. The next train bound for Midtown did indeed depart in twenty minutes. He could not wait that long. It wasn't the first metro he'd missed that night. The first had left without him back in Upper Manhattan where he attended university. Before that, his professor held him up at the lab.

Thomas checked his wristwatch. He could make it, but he would have to run fast. "Have a good night," he said to the woman.

Out in the chill night air, he jogged to the nearest street corner, hailed a cab, and joined the stream of bustling traffic that flowed through every part of the city. As the cab skirted and jerked through the column of cars, he kept a close eye on the time, his shoe tapping impatiently against the floor mats. Ten minutes later, the traffic jam had thickened and showed no sign of letting up soon. He was going to be late. Running on foot the remainder of the way seemed like the best option at this point.

"I'll just get out here," he told the cabbie. "Thanks."

Let out on the curb, Thomas ran. He ran all the way to Midtown—a twelve-minute sprint that left him winded, his shirt collar damp with sweat. He slowed to a brisk jog before a sorry apartment complex, naked of trees, with trash cans overturned outside and a busted street lamp. He was running again by the time he entered the building and headed down the hallway to his ground-floor apartment. He spotted his neighbor, Mrs. Dekker, waiting outside his door.

No. He didn't have time for this.

"Tom," she said, perking up. "I've been waiting—"

"I'm sorry, Mrs. Dekker," he intervened. "But I really haven't got the time tonight."

"Please. It'll only take a second. It's my back," she explained. "It still hurts and I can't lift trash bags into the dumpster."

Thomas checked his watch again and sighed. "Sure, I'll help," he agreed.

When he finally entered his apartment five minutes later, he had just enough time to tidy up the worst of the mess—to stuff a bundle of strewn clothes into a laundry basket and to rinse a stack of dirty dishes—before the doorbell rang. He spun around as the chime sounded through his small apartment, reverberating against his pounding heart. He peered through the spy hole. Outside in the hall stood one of his classmates, her dark hair tucked into a loose ponytail, her hands grasping a heavy red purse.

Thomas drew a steady breath. He loosened the collar of his shirt and then unfastened the bolts. She was scrolling through her phone when he greeted her. "Hey, Julie. Hope you found the place okay."

"Not really. Midtown isn't really a place I hang out. Too many creeps, you know?" She looked past his shoulder. "You gonna invite me in?"

He sidestepped quickly, showing her inside. "Yeah, sorry."

Still holding her phone, Julie took in the apartment with raised eyebrows. Twice he caught her inspecting the upswept floor and felt her disapproval palpably. He cleared his throat, unable to shake off the feeling of discomfort.

"Hey, I appreciate you taking a look at my term paper," she said, taking a seat at the kitchen table and switching on her phone to send a text message.

"It's no problem," Thomas assured. He pretended to glance over her term paper, which was lying face-up on the kitchen table, even though he'd already proofread it a dozen times and written a few suggestions at the bottom. He took the chair across from her, hoping to alleviate the awkward silence. "I was thinking," he said. "This might take a while. If you're hungry, maybe we could go out for some food later?"

"Like a date?" she asked.

Thomas smiled. "If you're okay with that, yeah. Or if you're not up for it tonight, how about Friday? There's a nice place I know on—"

"Look, I'm just going to tell you straight," she said. She sighed, her face still illuminated by the light of her phone screen as her fingers flew over the keys. "Don't take this the wrong way, Tom, but you're not really my type."

Abruptly his insides went cold. "Yeah," he managed. "Sure...I get it. No problem."

Julie stuffed her phone into her purse. She gave him a weak, almost imperceptible smile. "Look, I'm really sorry, but my friend needs my help with something. I gotta go. I'll pick up my paper at school when you're finished, okay?"

Thomas froze momentarily. She wanted to leave? A heavy feeling settled deep in the pit of his stomach. After a brief hesitation, he stood and opened the door to show her out.

"Just a tip, Tom," Julie said as she stepped into the hall. "If you're going to have a girl over, you could at least put on a clean shirt. And maybe clean your apartment."

"I had a busy day," he said.

"Still...the effort shows."

Heat flushed down his face, his neck. "Bye, Julie," was all he said.

She set off down the hallway, not bothering to return the farewell.

As illustrated in the scene above, some people choose to go about rejection in a cruel way. While rejection will never cease to be an uncomfortable experience, it doesn't have to be unfriendly or hostile. (Of course, if the young man is being aggressive in some way, a firm reaction is justified). However, if the young man approaches respectfully and in good faith, it doesn't take much of an effort to be kind, to show appreciation for the compliment of being asked on a date. If we girls fail to do so, we risk severely damaging a young man's self-esteem. Harsh words might even make him feel too insecure to ask other girls out in the future.

There is another aspect to rejection which I feel is important to mention: fear of carrying out rejection. A young man I know, Jordan, asked his girlfriend to marry him a few months ago. While I don't know Jordan's girlfriend, it's clear that he loved her at one point. Lately though, he's been having serious doubts about their upcoming marriage. But since he doesn't want to hurt the girl, he can't find it in his heart to break up with her. Instead, he's hoping that, by an act of divine intervention, she'll meet someone else and then break up with him. Obviously, this is the worst plan in the history of mankind. Not only is it completely unfair to the girl, but it's also unfair to him. Walking into a loveless marriage for the sake of protecting feelings is wrong. Of course, I and many others have advised Jordan to break up with the girl to no avail. Experiencing rejection is just as terrible for young men as it is for us girls, but in the end, the vast majority of us will be more grateful for a sincere relationship rather than a relationship with someone who is dating us simply to avoid hurting our feelings.

Even if we put romantic relationships aside, there are dozens of other areas of our lives where we might also be required to reject. Perhaps our colleagues or acquaintances are constantly asking us to help them in some way. Perhaps they need favors. Or perhaps they need emotional support. Wanting to be kind, we always say yes.

But as time passes, we start to get worn down. Our energy is being drained. As a result, we start to lag in the more important areas of our lives, such as our familial and romantic relationships, and our material and spiritual goals. Saying "no" is necessary at this point. While it's always good to help people, there's a limit, particularly because there are many people who will never stop asking for our help, no matter how often we give it.

Despite what some people may claim, rejection is not failure. Failure involves the active decision to despair, while rejection is simply a sign of redirection or an opportunity to improve. Ultimately though, it's up to us—whether it's us being rejected or us doing the rejecting—to consider carefully what we're being faced with. It's also up to us to decide how we're going to handle it.

4

"Courage is fire, and bullying is smoke."

—Benjamin Disraeli

What Bullying Is (And Is Not)

Nowadays, if you were to ask a crowd of people to define the term, "bullying," you'd likely get a hundred different replies. "Bullying is cruel words," one person might say. A second person might take their definition a bit further: "Bullying is criticism." And a third person might even go so far as to say, "Bullying is disagreement."

The reason you would receive such a broad definition of bullying is due to the increased hypersensitivity of current society. Certain groups have come to value emotions over logic and facts. They expect and even *demand* to be shielded from the slightest offense. They disregard the notion that being challenged by others is a positive thing—that it can make us mentally tougher and supply us with the tools to successfully debate our opinions.

Let's say that I publish a video on YouTube that took ten hours to film and edit, so I'm extremely proud of it. I can't wait to witness my audience's reaction to all of my hard work. The first comment arrives:

This video is awful. How can a person with as many subscribers as you allow herself to be so inaccurate? Next time, try being a little less lazy and take a look at the statistics. I'll even send you some sources.

The comment is harsh, but is it bullying? No, it's criticism. The major difference between criticism and bullying is that criticism recognizes what our end goal is and seeks to help us accomplish it. Bullying, on the other hand, seeks to insult us with no regard for our end goal.

Something else that current society often conflates with bullying is the act of disagreement. Imagine that you decide to see a movie at the theater with one of your friends. As you leave the theater, the movie finished, your friend is raving, telling you over and over about how much she enjoyed it.

"I didn't care for the movie," you say.

"What?" Your friend is stunned. "*How* could you not like it? It was directed by a woman."

"The fact that a woman directed the movie has nothing to do with why I didn't like it," you explain. "There are plenty of movies directed by women that I've enjoyed. I just found the dialogue in this one cliché. I also found the hero's character underwhelming."

"You're unbelievable," your friend scoffs. "We're supposed to *support* women. The reason there are so few female directors nowadays is because of people like *you*. You're a hater."

Muttering in anger, your friend stalks off.

Perhaps not all of us have experienced such an extreme situation, but we've likely experienced something similar. The era of "agreeing to disagree" is over. Society was not always this way, though. Once, we encouraged healthy debate. And even if we failed to reach common ground with one another, we were still able to maintain a sense of respect, even friendship.

Nowadays, disagreement is far too often likened to bullying and being a "hater." While disagreement can devolve into bullying if we insult or even threaten our opponents, for the most part, being able to disagree with each other is the natural state of a healthy society.

Why Bullies Bully

It was an unseasonably cold September. Clouds of low-forming mist had settled in the mountain foothills, giving the California countryside a haunted air.I remember hanging back in the kitchen after breakfast and telling my parents how crazy my life had become over the past two months. Political activism was not the simple life I'd anticipated. Day in and day out, I was being bombarded with messages, interview requests and invitations to speak at events. While I didn't necessarily enjoy receiving such attention—particularly the negative attention—I found enthusiasm and strength in the belief that I was fighting a good fight.

Still wearing my pajamas, a cup of coffee in hand, I returned to my room where I took some time to check my new messages: on Twitter, on Facebook, on YouTube, on Instagram, and lastly, my two separate public emails. (Yeah, I had two public emails; that's how crazy things got.)

Not all of the messages were positive. *You're a hateful whore*, some wrote. *You'd better hope I don't run into you on the street*, said others. But these types of messages didn't bother me in the way they once had. I'd learned to desensitize myself to the attacks of my opponents. Thick skin was a requirement when it came to politics.

What made today different, though, was a cryptic-looking email with the subject line, *I'm coming for you*. Unsurprisingly, the body of the email was worse.

Think twice about going out alone anymore, you vile bitch. Your family, too. I'm coming to kill you all.

At the bottom of the email, the person had posted my home address.

I'd been doxed.

Somehow, my personal information had been hacked and leaked online, meaning that for the first time, the possibility of a person following through on their threat was real.

I stopped leaving the house alone. I stopped my daily runs around the neighborhood and I stopped going to local cafes to work. I even began sleeping with a loaded gun beside my bed. When I warned my family about the message, they took it seriously, but of course they could only do so for so long—eventually, they had to move on with their lives. I was scared for my sisters every time one of them went out alone.

It took me nearly two months to realize that reacting so drastically to threats wasn't sustainable. I couldn't go on the defensive every time my inbox lit up with a hostile message. If so, I would never leave my house. At this point, both my health and productivity were suffering. I had allowed the vague threats of anonymous opponents to box me in. I knew I had to stop living in fear. In a way, this decision forced me to desensitize myself to death. As I became more popular, the likelihood increased that someone would show up at my house or at a public event and attack me.

The threats against my family, on the other hand, were something I was never able to come to terms with. Had one of my siblings ended up hurt, I would've felt responsible. Eventually, my family left California and moved to a safer state, which made me feel a lot better, but sometimes I still get the feeling it would be safer for them if I didn't visit home.

In the long run, I, and many other girls, will never see an end to certain people's attacks because their hatred isn't truly of us—it's a hatred of our beliefs. And since our beliefs aren't something we're likely to surrender, the only way for us to live a normal life is to make peace with the fact that hatred and possibly even violence is the price for our principles.

People will choose to bully us for a multitude of other reasons. Some people might bully us because they're in a position of power; they have a strong urge to constantly wield their power over us so that we never forget who's in charge. Other people might bully us because they have family issues at home. Maybe they have bad parents who are abusing them, or perhaps they even have a history of social rejection themselves. In this respect, they might consider bullying us as a means to retake power, a way to mitigate their own insecurities. Tormented by a need to feel dominant, they push us down in order to lift themselves up.

Another motivation for bullying is when people feel betrayed. I've experienced bullying for this reason, although I've never talked about it publicly until now...

Aside from myself, about a dozen or so other female activists exist in our political network. Most of these girls advocate for a return to traditionalism—not in an extreme way of course, just standard traditional values such as strong family units, celebration of motherhood and fatherhood, and so on. Many of the young men in our political network also claim to believe in these values, so for a time, life was drama-free.

Then one day, out of the blue, someone posted private information on the internet concerning one of the girls in my network, claiming that the information proved she had a long history of not living up to the values she preached. Although the information was from the past—meaning the girl might've considerably changed since then—it didn't matter. In the eyes of the young men in our network, she was a liar and a hypocrite. All hell broke loose.

Fueled by their anger, they set out on a mission to uncover similar information relating to *all* of the girls in our network. They recruited help from thousands of anonymous social media accounts, with the end goal being to prove that none of us were sincere—that all of us were manipulative whores whose grand scheme was to take advantage of our audiences. They fanned the flames by publishing a stream of posts and videos on the internet, accusing us over and over and over of being "liars" and "hoes who just want money."

Personally, I never understood this criticism. If all of us were soulless, if our primary goal in life were to make money, we would've pursued alternative careers. Political activism doesn't pay as much as some people might think, at least not for most of us. Moreover, almost any other career would be less mentally stressful and more physically safe.

The drama really kicked into overdrive when the mainstream media got involved. Various outlets reached out to us for comments and received no reply. We believed they'd misrepresent the situation and chose not to accept their interview requests. They went on to publish the stories anyway, and sure enough, all were misrepresentative.

To be honest, I don't know all the details of the drama that unfolded during this time. I chose to log off of social media at the first sign of a storm. However, a few of the girls targeted by the attacks set up a direct message group as a way to encourage one another, which I did participate in for a short time. Most of the girls were taking it a lot harder than me. Crying. Depression. Panic Attacks.

I can't do this anymore, one girl wrote.

I just want to go get married and have kids, wrote another.

Me too, someone agreed. *I hate political activism. The only reason I stick it out is because our cause is one worth fighting for.*

I can deal with our opponents' attacks, but not attacks from our own side, someone else added.

Overall, the attitude was grim. Many of the girls wanted to give up politics altogether.

I briefly considered quitting as well. Not because political activism was too difficult, but because if the standard for advocating for a better world was perfection, then I'd already failed. I'm not perfect. In fact, I'm far from it. I haven't always made the moral choice, and I've had to face the consequences for it. But on that note, I've never once claimed to be unflawed or above others.

Take a moment to think about all the mistakes you've made throughout the course of your life. All the let-downs, all the insincerities and all the screw-ups. Now apply your imperfections to everyone else in the entire world. This is a more realistic conception of humanity. The difference between the good people and the bad people is that the good people keep trying.

After about a week of feeling sorry for myself, I finally admitted that, in my state, quitting politics would be an emotional decision rather than a logical one. I put the past behind me and started making videos again. I never spoke publicly about or even acknowledged anything that had happened. Instead, I chose to look at it as another part of the battle.

It was not right—and certainly not kind—that the girls in our network had been treated like that, but despite disagreeing with most of the young men's accusations, I support their right to have made them. As long as a person doesn't advocate for or incite violence, I believe they have every right to speak. No matter how unjust their words might be, a world without freedom of speech would be far more unjust.

While there are numerous other motivations for bullying, in my personal experience, when girls bully, most of them do it out of jealousy, or because they consider their target as competition. The moment they've determined someone to be a threat, they zero in and attack, thinking that if they neutralize their target, they can more easily acquire their goal.

I attended college in a small Kansas town—so small that I could walk the length of it in about thirty minutes. Since the punishment for bullying at my college was suspension, there were no real instances where this occurred. Unfortunately, the same rules didn't apply to the public school on the opposite side of town.

A group of three girls who attended this public school detested me. For the first few months of college, they stalked me whenever I was out and about the town, yet refrained from confronting me face-to-face. Instead, they patrolled the streets in their car, windows rolled down, shouting out comments to me like "whore" and "bitch." I was confused. I didn't know where the girls' hatred came from, for I'd never spoken to, much less met, any of them before. It wasn't until a few months later that I learned the reason for their bullying.

Ever since I was little, my family has been close with another family that has extremely beautiful daughters and extremely handsome sons. One of the sons, Sebastian, reconnected with me when I arrived back in town for college. We quickly became good friends, often walking around town together and talking.

As it turned out, one of the three girls who hated me had a huge crush on Sebastian. She'd seen us walking together a few times and had feared we were dating. This is why, as soon as she discovered that I wasn't interested in Sebastian in a romantic way, the threat I posed to her vanished. The insults stopped. Even crazier, the girls started talking to me. I remember them pulling up to me in their car one afternoon as I was walking to the local supermarket.

"Cute boots," one of the girls said.

I was a bit skeptical, but still responded, "Thanks."

"Where'd you get them?" Another girl asked.

"At a mall back in California."

"You have nice style."

And then the girls sped off, car tires kicking up snow and slush. I never heard from any of them again. What a bizarre experience.

From Victim to Victor

As demonstrated in my story about cyberbullying, I think one of the most helpful methods to overcome verbal attacks is through establishing a support network. Family. Friends. Even a school counselor, therapist or priest. Perhaps some of us are hesitant to confide, while others are closed to the idea. But in my experience, isolation is the absolute worst response to bullying. In detaching ourselves from family and friends, we become easy prey.

I like to consider myself a relatively laid-back person. I don't often cry—I try to never do so in public. Over the past ten years, I've cried about eight times, and all but two of those times occurred within the past two years.

The worst of these instances occurred during the first six months of my political activism. I'd failed to give myself a break or a proper night's sleep since I started. Day after day, the stress from being constantly terrorized had built up to the point where my mental and emotional state was corroding, like a sheet of metal left out in the rain.

I remember my twin sister holding my hand as, for the first time in my life, I suffered a panic attack. Crying. Shortness of breath. Sweating. It was as if my skin had become as heavy as stone and was folding in on me, crushing my chest and lungs. I truly thought I was having a heart attack. Worst of all was the complete numbness that spread through my hands and face. I felt paralyzed. Anyone who has ever suffered a panic attack will agree that it's a terrifying experience. For me, it was an "out-of-body episode," like watching myself from somewhere else in the room. I've never felt so weak and helpless.

Up to this point, I'd trained myself to be capable of overcoming a lot, but I couldn't do it on my own this time. I needed my mother and twin sister to care for me—to talk to me, to encourage me, sometimes to just sit in comforting silence with me.

Most of us will need similar support every now and again and it's nothing to be ashamed of. Showing vulnerability to our loved ones is natural. Moreover, allowing ourselves to be vulnerable deepens our relationships and strengthens our bonds. Telling our loved ones we don't need their help is equivalent to telling them we don't need them—that we don't value their support. Not to mention, it's not as if loved ones regard helping as a chore. They want to be there for us and are simply waiting for us to ask.

The question of showing vulnerability to the world, on the other hand, is entirely different. Perhaps doing so might work for some of us. Unfortunately, I can rarely afford to do so. I have too many opponents, circling me like wolves, waiting to take me down at the first sign of weakness.

The best option in this case is to treat our aggressors with indifference. Even if their words hurt us, we should pretend not to care one way or the other. We should appear neutral on the matter. The reason this approach often works is because our aggressors are seeking a reaction. Their ultimate goal is to get a rise out of us. Without winning a reaction of anger or sadness, they lose out on the satisfaction of a follow through, which eventually might cause them to grow bored, perhaps even leave us alone.

A few other good options are to react with kindness or humor. In the case of kindness, if we are sincere, it might push our aggressors to experience remorse and reevaluate their behavior. In the case of humor, if we conceal our vulnerability and reject the bait that our aggressors so desperately want us to take, we'll maintain our position of power.

The mainstream media writes hit pieces about me on a regular basis. But a certain hit piece written by a British newspaper a few months ago takes the cake. The hit piece referred to me in a degrading manner, calling me a "Barbie Fiancée." Worse, it outright accused me of committing crimes such as attempting to drown innocent people in the Mediterranean. You can imagine how shocked I was as I read the article, for I've never once advocated for violence in my life. On the contrary, I've only ever advocated for peaceful political activism. Not to mention, if I'd truly committed the crimes that the hit piece accused me of, I wouldn't be writing this book right now—I'd be sitting in a jail cell.

Obviously, I couldn't afford to ignore the hit piece. But since suing the mainstream media is very expensive and rarely successful, I decided that the best course of action was to respond with humor. I made a video in which I became the Barbie Fiancée they'd accused me of being, acting like an airheaded ditz while debunking all of their salacious claims. Naturally, the video made the British newspaper look stupid, but more importantly, the vast majority of people who viewed the video took my side. While reacting with humor doesn't always work out the way we want it to, depending on the situation, it can be an extremely useful tool when it comes to combating our aggressors.

Why You Don't Want the Bully to Be You

One of the most important people in the world to me, a girl named Daisy, used to share an apartment with a roommate. One night, Daisy told her roommate she was going on a date with her boyfriend and that she would probably return home late. However, at the last minute, she decided to stay home because she was feeling sick. The roommate, still thinking Daisy had gone out, invited a few girlfriends over for some wine and all of them got to talking. Soon, the talking turned to gossip. Eventually, the gossip turned to the topic of Daisy.

"Why does *every* single guy in town seem to like Daisy?" the roommate complained from where she sat on the sofa. "It's so annoying."

"Yeah, for one thing, she's way too skinny," a second girl agreed.

"I bet you she's bulimic," a third girl suggested. "At the very *least*, she's anorexic."

"It's really ugly," the roommate said. "I honestly have no idea what the guys see in her. Plus, I don't think she's nearly as nice as she pretends to be."

"It's definitely fake," the second girl concluded. "I know a bitch in nice-girl-clothing when I see one."

Daisy, who had overheard the girls' conversation from her bedroom, was deeply hurt. She was shocked to hear the real opinions of her friends. Words like this had never been spoken to her face. As the night wore on, eventually the roommate made the humiliating discovery that Daisy had indeed been home all along. Too afraid to apologize in person, she scrawled a note of apology and left it on Daisy's bedroom door. Despite feeling betrayed, Daisy forgave her roommate. Daisy sensed that the bitter words of those girls had originated from the insecurities that every girl feels, not from a place of malice.

How many of us have caved to our insecurities and bullied other girls at one point or another—whether that girl be a stranger, a friend or even our sister or mother? Granted, it's sometimes extremely difficult to be nice to certain people, but what helps is reminding ourselves of how being bullied makes us feel—how deeply it bruises our pride and negates our sense of self-worth. Some girls are incredibly sensitive; it takes them years to overcome bullying, and if we're the ones guilty of bullying them, their pain is our responsibility.

On that note, we aren't the only gender affected by bullying. Whether we realize it or not, from a young age, boys also have the capacity to take offense. The reason some of us might overlook this fact is because most boys repel vulnerability. They act unaffected, as if our disparaging words evaporate upon coming into contact with their ears. But this is almost never the case. Cruel words and actions *do* affect them.

Consider the types of messages being directed at boys today. In our homes, at our schools, at our workplaces, and even in our entertainment, the dominant culture tells boys that they alone are responsible for all of society's problems. "Boys are the oppressors and girls are the oppressed," is the general consensus. The dominant culture tells boys that, due to their gender, they are automatically privileged; that they've been oppressing girls for far too long and that the "future is female" now; that their inherent tendency towards masculinity and rowdiness is toxic; that all of them are potential rapists; that, in the case of rape accusations, girls should alwaysbe believed; that boys don't have a right to due process, and instead, should be tried in the court of public opinion.

Granted, some boys, young and old, are tyrants. Some are criminals, abusers, rapists and so on. But not all are this way. In fact, most *aren't* this way.

Think about the average boy attending middle school or high school. He's mainly concerned with friends, video games, sports and his grades—all in all, he's very normal. But if he's constantly being beaten down by attacks such as "all boys are toxic," how is he ever supposed to grow into a man? As the dominant culture continues to label him worthless for deceitful reasons outside his control, his method of coping might turn to resentment and anger. Worse, he might even start to believe the messages being directed at him. "I'm automatically worthless, so what's the point of trying?"

A boy who feels this way will generally turn to escapism:

increased video gaming, comic books, internet forums and
YouTube. And since the dominant culture has made him too
uncomfortable to approach real girls, he might even replace us as
he gets older with porn or sex robots.

The fact that boys feel this way growing up is also why we're
now seeing so many "male-only" groups forming: *Men's Rights
Activists, Men Going Their Own Way*, and so on. Young men are
opting out of marriage, of having children, and even of allowing
themselves to love—all because they believe women can no longer
be trusted. "Sooner or later, every woman will betray us," they say.
"They'll divorce us, take our children and our money. Women
aren't capable of love; they're only capable of loving what we can
give them."

I've seen the ugliness of the ever-growing gender divide
firsthand. Girls who believe that all young men are oppressors and
that sticking up for them is wrong have condemned and ridiculed
me. And young men who believe that all girls are manipulative
parasites who can't be trusted have slandered and bullied me. On
both fronts, the attacks hurt, but why should I have expected
anything different? The overall trust between girls and boys has
been decimated.

Society will reward us for bullying our male counterparts. For
blaming and belittling them. For accusing and judging them. But
the truth is, if we ever want to return to the days when we had
communities full of healthy boys and men, first we're going to

have to return to respecting them in the way that we once did. When I say "respect," I don't mean all-out adoration of every random male we come into contact with. I mean respect in the sense that, at the very least, we should give them the benefit of the doubt; we should refrain from painting them as bad simply because they're male, never mind whether they've actually done anything bad. Whether we realize it or not, the majority of girls of all ages want to be loved, while the majority of boys of all ages want to be respected—not just by girls, but by other boys as well.

If you don't believe me, try telling your boyfriend, husband, brother or father that you respect him, and when you do so, be specific about the ways in which you respect him. If he doesn't believe you, he might not produce the desired reaction. But if you try again, and are able to convince him that you're sincere, his reaction might be unlike anything you've seen from him before: he might be happier, kinder and more loving; he might feel more confident and more motivated; and best of all, you will have given him a genuine moment of feeling accepted, appreciated and admired.

To give another example: Why is it that many young men today think we're interested in dating them if we simply give them a compliment? Perhaps we didn't even compliment them in a flirtatious way, but for some reason it makes them think we're interested. This is because most of them are rarely given compliments by people outside their circle of family, friends and girlfriends. So when an outsider compliments them—especially if the outsider is a girl—the last thing on their mind is that we simply want to be kind.

I'm not claiming that girls alone are to blame for the state of the gender divide. Some individual girls are responsible and some are not. Some individual boys are responsible and some are not. No gender is fully at fault. In general, it's the fault of the dominant culture, which is constantly fanning the flames of the war. In the end, it's going require the efforts of both genders to fix the problem, but for this to happen, one gender has to take the first step. Even if we as individual girls are not part of the problem, we can be part of the solution.

5

"An echo has no voice of its own."

—Marty Rubin

How We Fake Ourselves Out

You're enjoying a night out at Vicky's parents' vacation home, a two-story log cabin tucked away on a forested mountain ridge. Out on the porch, the winter air flushes your face; a fire crackles and blazes in a circle of gray rocks. Huddled close for warmth, wrapped in a blanket, you steal a glance at Vicky, thinking how strange it was to receive an invitation. You haven't spoken much before tonight. She's one of the most popular girls at your high school. Another girl named Gemma is there too—pretty, with a pert nose and a carefree vibe. She sits with her boots close to the fire, and every so often, sips from a flask in her purse. You don't know her well either. All you know is that you're eager to befriend both girls.

"You're going out with Liam now, right?" Vicky asks you. Eyes fixed to her phone, she awaits your response with divided attention.

A tremor of unease flows through you. Given that you've only just started seeing Liam, you don't want to discuss the relationship.

"It's nothing official," you answer, spearing a marshmallow on the end of a stick and holding it over the fire. "He hasn't asked me to be his girlfriend yet."

"Lucky," Gemma says, lighting up a cigarette. "Literally the worst mistake you could make is committing to a guy while you're still young. You should take it easy and have fun for a while—at least until you're twenty-five."

You disagree with Gemma. But before you have a chance to respond, Vicky asks, "Have you guys had sex yet?"

"Uh...." You pause, surprised and caught off guard. "No...not yet."

Were Liam and I supposed to have sex already? you wonder. Up to this point, you had decided to wait to have sex until getting married. Or at the very least, you wanted to wait for the right guy, someone you love.

Gemma blows a smoke ring at the fire. "Why not? What's the problem?"

"Well...you know..." Weighed down by the pressure, you

momentarily lose your train of thought. "I guess...I guess it's because I don't love him."

Vicky laughs. She still hasn't looked your way; her face remains tilted towards her phone, a smirk pinching the corner of her mouth. "Who cares about love. Right now, when you're young, you're supposed to have sex with as many guys as possible. How else do you expect to have fun and to become sexually confident? Once you're in a committed relationship or married, then you're stuck with the same guy forever. Your chance for new experiences is over."

You pull your marshmallow out of the fire and set the stick on a nearby table, no longer in the mood to eat. Although your resolve is weakening, you manage a final protest. "Liam and I have only gone on three dates. I barely know him."

"Wow." Gemma rolls her eyes. "Didn't realize you were such a prude. Three dates, one date...who cares...sex isn't a big deal."

"She's right," Vicky agrees. "The only reason there's a stigma around sex is because of people like you."

A flush burns up your face; you avoid eye contact. Despite having different beliefs from Vicky and Gemma, you know there's nothing wrong with your way of thinking. In fact, you are certain yours are good principles to live by. The problem is that you still want Vicky and Gemma to approve of you. It's difficult to make friends at school. Plus, if you disagree with them, there's a chance they might tell other girls at school that you're a prude. It might become harder to make friends.

"Liam and I have already had sex," you suddenly say. "I only pretended that we hadn't because I thought you girls might be the judgy type."

Vicky raises her eyebrows, impressed. She finally puts down her phone. "Get it, girl. That's a record, even for us."

Gemma smiles and flicks her cigarette butt into the fire. "Wow. You're really not as uptight as I thought you were."

Relief hits you, as if a great weight has suddenly lifted off your shoulders. You smile. Acceptance feels good...praise feels even better. The fact that you've put on a new face to please the girls bothers you a little, but eventually, you decide it doesn't matter.

If you're a girl who's found herself in a similar situation, you're one of many. A lot of us wear more than one face, or at the very least, we've worn more than one face in the past. We have a natural ability to read people, situations and environments and to change faces depending on how we believe we'll best fit in. Of course, it's not that we deliberately want to be fake, per se, it's that we have an inexorable desire to be loved and accepted.

These desires are completely normal, and when kept under control, are nothing to be ashamed of. The danger of these desires comes when we act upon them, becoming insincere chameleons in the process. Moreover, if we're willing to fundamentally change ourselves for the sake of one person, what's to say we won't change for everyone? We'll end up developing hundreds of different personalities, physical appearances, and sets of beliefs in our effort to succeed. Of course, even then, our attempts will likely fail.

1st Way We End Up Fake:
We Know Ourselves But Act Like We Don't

One of the major causes of inauthenticity—as illustrated in the story above—is when we know ourselves, but choose to betray our principles in an effort to fit in. We might even be pressured by people to the point of hearing phrases like, "If you don't agree with me, then you're a loser," or "If you don't agree with me, then you're a bad person."

Naturally, these sorts of statements can shake us. They threaten us with the label of "outcast." They put tremendous pressure on us to renounce our principles, to surrender our authenticity and to mold ourselves in accordance with the people we wish to be accepted by. These types of situations become even more distressing when we know we're in the right, not just factually, but ethically as well.

Doing the right thing is almost never easy. In fact, doing the right thing is oftentimes the loneliest and most difficult option. It's the unpaved path, shrouded in trees and darkness. In situations such as these, it can sometimes be helpful to take a step back. We should give ourselves a short timeout period, during which we can put our emotions aside and closely examine who we are and what we believe. If, at the end of our deliberation, we decide that we are in the right, we ignore what others think. We battle on.

If we're unable to battle on, though—if every now and then we cave to inauthenticity—this doesn't necessarily make us fake. The major difference between authentic and inauthentic girls is that authentic girls refuse to ever fully surrender to inauthenticity. If they notice themselves stumbling, they regain their balance. They try to correct their mistake.

For eight years—from age fifteen to twenty-three—I was a part of the writing industry. Back then, I wrote science-fiction and fantasy books for young adults. Most of you are likely already familiar with the young adult genre, for it produced international hits such as *The Hunger Games*.

During my spare time, when I wasn't writing or working a job as a nanny, I attended dozens of writing seminars and conventions hoping to meet and befriend fellow authors. The experience was disheartening to say the least. I quickly came to realize that none of the other authors shared my beliefs—not personal, political or religious. On the contrary, they openly condemned my stance. One thing I can say about the writing industry is that it's always moving and changing, like a river, always rushing in pursuit of the next politically correct narrative. You won't find a more sterile and politically correct environment, except perhaps at university. I think it goes without saying that my opinions were not politically correct. So I was forced to keep all of my beliefs hidden or risk being ostracized. I had witnessed this happen to several other authors in the past, and I didn't want it to happen to me—not only because I knew I might lose my chance at the acceptance I so desperately wanted, but because I knew I might also lose my chance at being published by a traditional publishing house.

So I chose the coward's way out: I kept silent. I refrained from sharing my personal, political or religious beliefs in an effort to fit in. I wanted to please the other authors and have them accept me in return. Doing so made me feel the opposite of how I'd anticipated. Instead of feeling joy from acceptance, I felt misery. As time wore on, I experienced an ever-increasing sense of loneliness. I knew I was betraying my principles and felt cheapened in doing so. Even though I wasn't verbally agreeing with the other authors in conversations, keeping silent was the equivalent of telling them that their views were the right ones.

Letting go of my desire to be accepted by the writing industry took five long years. What eventually changed my mind, thrusting me back into reality, was when I decided to read all the top books on the New York Times Bestseller's List.

You can imagine my surprise when, after checking out the top books from my local library and reading them, I realized that I didn't like them. In fact, most of them would have fit well in a trash bin. The majority of the authors' arguments, both thematic and moral, were lacking. It disturbed me that these writers (mostly women) had been given such power to influence the youth, for they glorified themes like verbal and emotional abuse, rejection of authority and female supremacy. Some of them even glorified violence, revenge and murder. Moreover, none of their characters were in line with what I aspired to be—in fact, most of the characters, even the heroes, were in stark conflict with my idea of goodness.

This was the moment I realized that, if the day ever came when these authors truly accepted me, it would only be because I allowed myself to become one of them. While, even at this point, it remains difficult to fully let go of my desire for acceptance in the writing industry, I know that living out my dream as a sellout would be even more difficult.

2nd Way We End Up Fake:
We Don't Know Ourselves But Act Like We Do

Another major cause of inauthenticity stems from not knowing ourselves. We aren't confident in who we are, what we believe and what we hope to accomplish. As a result, we mimic those around us, adopting their personalities, their aspirations, their likes and dislikes, and even their political and religious beliefs. Sometimes, doing so might not bother us in the moment because, in not knowing ourselves, mimicking others doesn't feel inauthentic. In fact, it might even feel like a discovery of our true selves. But this is rarely the case.

When we ignore the development of our true selves for the sake of acceptance, sooner or later, even if it's years down the road, we'll eventually notice a hole in our souls. We won't know how to fill the hole, only that it needs to be filled. Not knowing how to fill the hole might cause us to ignore it, and if we do so for too long, we might lose the ability to find our true selves altogether. Our true selves will become nothing more than a distant "what if" from the past that we rejected. In this case, it will be near-impossible for us to ever be happy or to attain fulfillment. Even worse, no one will ever be able to love us for who we truly are. They'll only be able to love us for who we pretend to be.

During the first two years of high school, having no idea who I was or what I wanted, I molded myself to fit in with the popular crowd. Within the first few months of my arrival, I was one of the most popular girls in school. For about two years, I continued on this path. I was unhappy, but was unable to connect the dots as to why. My confused state led me to believe that my unhappiness was a result of my parents' and siblings' failure to understand me. "There's no use even trying to explain anything to them," I told myself. "They aren't capable of understanding anyway."

During the summer following my sophomore year, when my mother had grounded me for three months, I finally found the answers I'd been searching for.

Initially, being confined to my room for several hours each day was torture. I had no laptop to surf the internet or watch movies, only a small iPod with about one-hundred songs on it. I considered reading, but decided I wasn't a fan after the first day. While I'd loved reading as a child, and I love it now, the popular crowd hadn't cared much for reading. In trying to fit in with them, I'd convinced myself that I didn't like it either.

My final option was to entertain myself. But since I'd allowed my mind to become a foreign place to me, entertaining myself was easier said than done. Obviously, this is a big red flag. We should never feel like a stranger in our own mind; we should know it inside out and backwards; we should feel some kind of unification with it.

The first few steps of my transition were jarring and difficult. I had to force myself to reject outside distractions. I had to force myself to endure the silence. But once I succeeded in doing so, I was finally able to hear my own mind. The result was an overwhelming feeling of comfort and relief, like reuniting with an old friend. For the first time since I could remember, I came to enjoy listening, thinking, creating, and so on. And from this, I was able to recognize that my unhappiness hadn't been caused by my family's inability to understand me, but as a symptom of inauthenticity.

For all of us who don't know ourselves, choosing to spend time alone is generally a good idea. Unburdened by outside influence and expectation, we'll have a far more peaceful journey of internal exploration and discovery. We'll have the freedom to try new things and to uncover what we respond to, what we hope to accomplish and what we believe.

3rd Way We End Up Fake
We Focus on Beauty (But Not Real Beauty)

The third major cause of inauthenticity arises when we allow ourselves to believe our true self is worthless. If we can't see our own value, it's generally because we believe we're physically ugly or because our minds and skills are undeveloped. For instance, it's been scientifically proven that the rational part of our brains doesn't fully develop until age twenty-five. As for our unique skills, they oftentimes don't have natural value; they gain value when we work to improve them. So as long as we're constantly making that effort, we won't think ourselves worthless. The belief that we're physically ugly, on the other hand, is a far more difficult battle to overcome.

I was overweight in high school. Even after losing the excess weight, I continued to grapple with the feeling that I was fat. In an effort to hide my body, I wore baggy pants and sweatshirts until I was nearly twenty.

Around this time, I also made the mistake of dyeing my hair with henna dye, which destroyed my hair for three years. I'd initially wanted to dye my hair dark brown, but the dye turned it black with a horrific greenish-bluish hue. The beauticians at the hair salon dyed my hair seven different times, trying anything they could to save it, but nothing worked. The only option was to chop my hair off and wait for it to grow out from the roots. I was heartbroken. I'd always loved long dark brown hair, but now I had short black hair. Worse, my complexion was washed out by the black hair, for it's naturally very pale—so pale that I can't remain in the sun for more than a few minutes without burning. Everyone at my high school thought I was going through a goth phase and started calling me "the vampire."

If I showed you a photo of me from my teenage years beside a photo of me now, you probably wouldn't believe it's the same person. In fact, oftentimes when I've traveled abroad, the border police have questioned whether the photo on my passport is truly me.

The point is, I can relate to feeling physically ugly. Much of my younger years were stained with a lack of self-worth that was born from a dislike of my body and face. Coming to terms with our physical appearances can oftentimes be a lifelong battle, even for the prettiest girls, and this is mainly because of the unrealistic standards we're presented with on a daily basis.

How many times have you been scrolling through Instagram and come across an advertisement using a beautiful celebrity? She appears perfect. But the reality is that the photo has almost always been through multiple rounds of photoshop—making the celebrity's body thinner, brightening her hair, straightening her teeth, removing all the blemishes from her skin, and even enlarging certain body parts like eyes and breasts. Furthermore, most celebrities spend thousands upon thousands of dollars on cosmetic surgery. Their gift of physical beauty isn't a natural one. Many of us believe it is, though. And so we continue striving for an unrealistic standard that we'll never attain—with the result being a loss of self-worth.

We might not always be as pretty as the girl standing next to us, but ways of improving do exist. We can grow our hair long, or style it in a way that better compliments our facial structure. We can whiten our teeth or straighten them with braces. We can enhance our faces using makeup. We can work hard to get in great physical shape.

That being said, physical beauty is far from the most important goal a girl can achieve in life. Think about all the beautiful girls and young men you've seen with less attractive partners. What made the attractive person decide to date or even to marry the less attractive person?

One reason might be for the person's reputation, or even for their money, but in the vast majority of cases, these relationships end in breakups or divorce. The relationships that last are the ones where the partners are drawn to each other's character.

Take, for example, a girl who has a beautiful appearance but an ugly character. Few of us would want to risk being friends with her. And whether we realize it or not, few young men would want to risk being with her either. Of course, many of them might pursue her initially—because they're attracted to her and want to have sex with her—but after a few one-night stands or even a short-term relationship, they'll walk away. They won't pursue a marriage with her, or even a long-term relationship, because the risk of being used, abused and cheated on is too great.

In the end, a young man will almost always choose a girl who makes up for what she lacks in outer beauty with what she possesses in inner beauty. Sincerity. Kindness. Generosity. Loyalty. Courage. Selflessness. He knows that a girl who has these types of qualities is a girl who will not only make his life happy, but a girl who he'll want to spend his life making happy.

At its core, physical beauty is obviously a great blessing. But physical beauty can be an even greater curse if we allow it to become our dominant quality. Perhaps we don't allow it to become our dominant quality intentionally; perhaps we do so because we're constantly being told how pretty we look. We consider physical beauty our crowning glory, and as a result, are constantly working to look our best, which ultimately risks us failing to develop any further good qualities or skills. In this case, when the inevitable day comes that our physical beauty starts to fade, so does our happiness.

The truth is that a girl who allows physical beauty to become her dominant quality is oftentimes the most insecure. Since her sense of self-worth is built upon appearance, whenever a more beautiful girl comes along, or even if she's simply having a bad hair day, her sense of self-worth is shattered. On the other hand, it's absolutely possible for girls who are beautiful on the outside to also be beautiful on the inside.

No girl is naturally great, but all of us have the *potential* to be great. The choice regarding whether we're willing to put in the necessary work to develop our potential, possibly attaining greatness in the process, is something we have to decide for ourselves.

How We Let Others Fake Us Out

Like me, Lily was a writer. One of her favorite pastimes was to visit her local bookstore and browse the best-seller aisle. Shiny and perfectly packaged, the books had managed to attain the stamp of approval that Lily's heart ached for. Her dream was to one day visit the bookstore and see a story of her own in the best-seller aisle. The problem was, apart from her family and close friends, no one complimented her stories. "You definitely have potential as a writer," strangers told her, "but you still have a long way to go."

Over time, Lily grew frustrated with hearing the same criticism. *Can't I just meet one person who likes my stories as much as I do?* she thought. *Are they really so bad?*

One day, while out to breakfast with her friend, Brianna, Lily got her wish.

"I gave a copy of your book to a relative of mine," Brianna said. "Last night, she called me up and told me she's really enjoying it."

Lily forgot the ham and eggs on her plate. She coughed as she fought to swallow her food and speak at the same time. "Who is it?" she gasped.

"Her name is—" Brianna paused, seeming reluctant to continue. "Her name is Carmen," finally came the answer. "I should warn you, though. She's a bit of a dark horse."

Lily disregarded the warning. The only thing she wanted to hear was how to contact Carmen. For the first time in her life, a stranger was enjoying her book. Could it really be true? Lily imagined that she and Carmen shared a rare connection. At the very least, Carmen was capable of seeing something that others couldn't see.

The minute Lily returned home, she contacted Carmen over social media.

Brianna told me you're enjoying my book. She typed out the message, hands wringing in anticipation, and then pressed "send."

Did the message sound too desperate? Maybe Carmen didn't love the book; maybe she only liked it. Maybe Lily was getting worked up over nothing.

Beep.

A new message. Carmen had already responded.

Oh my gosh, I can't believe it's you! I love your book so much! I stayed up all night to finish it. I've already started reading it a second time.

Lily smiled and stared at the computer screen...blinking once...blinking twice...hardly believing that the words she was seeing were real. Clearly, her first instinct about Carmen had been correct: they shared a rare connection.

A few weeks passed. As Lily got to know Carmen better, she was thrilled to discover how alike they were. They shared the same favorite food. They shared the same favorite fashion brand. They shared the same favorite historical figure. They also shared the same favorite books, music and movies. Somehow, they even shared the same personal, political and religious beliefs.

Despite their almost too many similarities, Lily loved Carmen. She believed that having such a friend was a once in a lifetime opportunity. Her only complaint was that Carmen constantly needed to spend time together and talk.

"She has no shame about calling me in the middle of the night," Lily complained to her mother.

"Maybe she's going through a lonely period and simply needs a friend," her mother responded.

Lily accepted her mother's advice. Perhaps seeing to a person's every personal whim was what good friends did. A few more weeks passed, and as they did so, Lily continued to feed Carmen's insatiable hunger for attention. On the outside, she did her best to appear happy, but on the inside, she could no longer deny the strain Carmen was putting on her mental health. She felt as if a parasite had attached itself to her brain and was slowly sucking the life out of her. Plus, she was growing a bit tired of their similarities. *Carmen doesn't seem to have even one unique trait of her own, Lily thought. How can two people possibly be so alike?*

Things took a turn for the worse when Carmen started to guilt-trip Lily. She claimed that Lily wasn't putting as much effort into her gifts, or that Lily wasn't there for her enough. During the launch party of Lily's now-published book, Carmen even accused Lily of ignoring her.

"I wasn't ignoring you," Lily defended. "Over three-hundred people were at the launch party. Not only did I have to thank each person individually, I also had to sign all of their books."

"That's not a good enough excuse," Carmen insisted. "I was a fan of your book long before any of those people." She pushed her hands over her eyes, as if trying to fight back tears. "What the launch party showed me is that the minute your book becomes popular, you're going to cast me aside. The only thing you really care about is writing."

Lily didn't know how to respond. Deep down, she knew that Carmen's accusations were unfair. The launch party was supposed to have been her day. She'd worked towards it for years, and if Carmen truly cared about her, she would've celebrated Lily's achievement instead of trying to make the achievement about her.

Now at her wits end, Lily sought advice from the girl who'd introduced her to Carmen in the first place."

"Something bad happened, didn't it?" Brianna guessed.

"Yes," Lily confessed. "I don't know how to explain it other than to use the word "obsessive." Carmen is never content with a part of my time. She wants *all* of it."

Brianna sat in silence for a while, a worried crease on her forehead. Finally she asked, "What's your favorite drink, Lily?"

Lily was unsure what the question had to do with Carmen, but answered, "Earl Grey Tea…with cream but no sweetener."

"And what's Carmen's favorite drink?"

"The same." An eerie sensation crept over Lily, as if she wasn't the first person to approach Brianna about Carmen.

"Have you…by chance…come to find that you share an unusual number of things in common with Carmen?" Brianna asked.

Lily almost leapt from her chair. At last, someone understood what she'd been going through. "Oh my gosh,yes. We have the same likes and dislikes in every area. It's almost creepy."

"Yes, it's creepy. And the creepiest part about it is that none of its real," Brianna explained. "You're not the first person Carmen has done this to. As far as I know, she's done it to three other people, but of course there might be more. It's why I tried to warn you about her. Carmen even pretended to be vegan and a Buddhist to impress her last boyfriend."

Lily felt her insides grow cold. Brianna's revelation meant that Carmen had never liked the same food, fashion brands, poetry, music, movies and books as she did. She likely wasn't religious or political either. Their entire friendship had been a ruse.

"Why...why does she pretend?" Lily asked.

Brianna shook her head. "I have no idea. Honestly, even though she's my cousin, I have no idea who the real Carmen is. She keeps her circle of friends small, constantly changing depending on the people she's with. The worst part is that it always ends badly. I'm so sorry, Lily. I never meant for this to happen."

Lily cut ties with Carmen that same day. Carmen protested at first, but then, as if realizing she'd been found out, vanished into thin air. To this day, I don't think Lily has heard from Carmen. I don't know if she ever discovered Carmen's motives for her actions either. For all I know, Carmen is currently out in the world inflicting the same strange torture on somebody else.

Most of us have met a fake girl or two. Perhaps we know one from our high school, university, job, or even from church. While choosing to keep our distance from these girls is perfectly justifiable, under certain circumstances, it might be worth it to try and help them. Not every fake girl is a manipulative schemer; some of them are simply confused. They haven't yet discovered who they are, or if they have, they've allowed themselves to become lost. Being a good friend and giving advice to these girls might help them to find or rediscover themselves.

That said, manipulative girls like Carmen also exist—girls who deliberately hide their true personality, and instead, show us a fake personality that they've specifically crafted in order to get close to us. In this case, as Lily did, it's best to cut ties.

There are also girls who pretend to like us, while secretly using us for their own gain, like a pawn in their personal game of chess. This is the type of girl who will abandon us as soon as she's gotten what she wants. Since she never liked us in the first place, she'll stop acknowledging our existence, at least until the time again comes when she needs something from us. In this case, it's also best to cut ties.

While Lily might've been able to help Carmen overcome her inauthenticity and tendency towards emotional manipulation if she'd worked very hard, there's an equal chance that she would've failed—and possibly even harmed herself in the process. Ultimately, it's up to us to determine whether or not a person is worth helping. The only thing for certain is that our help will never be worth it unless the person has a strong will to change.

Fake Change Versus Real Change

Choosing to change our character can oftentimes, but not always, be a negative act. The most important determining factor in such a decision is our level of sincerity.

When we abandon authenticity, our change is insincere, and more often than not, it's for a less than noble reason. For example, we make the decision to change ourselves without even considering whether it will make us a better person. We simply want to be accepted.

A moral character change, on the other hand, is always a positive act. For example, we notice severe flaws in our character. Wanting to become better people, we make a sincere effort to overcome these flaws. In this case, our character change will not only prove good for us, but for all the people in our lives.

Back when I was a nanny, I remember having a very interesting conversation with one of the little girls I used to care for, Rose. One day after school, Rose told me that she'd decided she wasn't going to be nice to a certain girl at her school anymore because she didn't like the girl and being nice to her would've meant she was being fake. I remember laughing, not because I thought Rose's words were funny, but because of the blunt way in which she'd spoken them. I also appreciated her black-and-white outlook of the world. I suppose most children have a similar outlook. I know I did.

I made sure to let Rose know that being kind to girls she didn't like wasn't fakeness; it was charity. I explained that she could only be considered fake if she was treating the girl kindly to her face, while at the same time, talking badly about her behind her back.

Authentic girls are like unique shades. We bring color to the world when we embrace our different personalities, appearances, ambitions and talents. Moreover, we're happier and more fulfilled existing with sincerity. Doing so might even pave the way for us to accomplish great things as wives, as mothers, and even as career professionals. But it's only through authenticity that we'll ever know.

6

"The mystery of human existence lies not in just staying alive, but in finding something to live for."

—Fyodor Dostoevsky

Finding Something to Live For

How old were you when you first had the desire to pursue a goal? I was five. I remember wandering into the kitchen to find my mother baking bread from scratch. Intrigued, I pushed a chair against the countertop and climbed on top for a better view. The way her hands kneaded the dough was smooth and effortless, honed through years of practice.

"Can I help?" I asked.

"Of course," my mother answered. "Why don't you make your own loaf?"

She tore off a small piece of dough and sprinkled it with flour.

I smiled as I kneaded the dough alongside her, making sure the shape and consistency was perfect. Once the dough had risen, my mother placed both loaves in the oven; I checked on mine every few minutes, making sure nothing bad had happened to it.

Ding.

I rushed toward the oven when the timer beeped, a pair of protective mitts over my hands. I'll never forget the satisfaction I felt as I removed my tiny loaf and placed it on the countertop. For the next few weeks, I wanted to be a mom, solely for the reason that I could make bread of my own. Granted, this dream faded after a little while. Over time, I developed new passions—interests inspired by my environment and by the people around me. The one constancy was that I always had a desire to do something specific.

Most of us have undergone similar stages in our youth. But even back then, somehow, we inherently understood that our purpose was like a map. Without it, we'd be destined to aimlessly wander the world forever, caught in an endless cycle of new paths and dead-ends.

The reason authenticity is so important is because it leads us to our purpose. Of course, in less common instances, some of us are able to find our true selves through executing our purpose, but for the most part, we have to know ourselves first. If we don't, we might end up falling into one of four traps, all of which lead to the same destination: regret.

1st Trap: Settling

We adopt another person's purpose as our own.

The primary pitfall of this trap is the fact that we'll never be able to love another person's purpose as much as our own—in the same way that we'll never be able to love another person's children as much as our own. A life purpose is often realized through internal trial and struggle, brought into focus by a person's own unique experiences and developed skills. True passion for a purpose can never successfully be faked or replicated. In most cases, if we adopt someone else's purpose, we won't particularly like or believe in that purpose. We might even start to feel unfulfilled or unhappy with our decision years down the road.

2nd Trap: Leapfrogging

We continually jump from purpose to purpose.

We think that we want to be a professional athlete, but a few years later, we change our minds and decide to pursue a career in fashion. From there, we switch to dancing, the culinary arts and then sculpting. On an endless loop the cycle continues. While we might accomplish small achievements here and there, we'll never experience the satisfaction of a follow-through. Our purposes will lie in the corner like unfinished books, collecting dust. The saddest ending to this type of scenario is when we do eventually discover our true purpose, but it's too late. In both cases, we look over our shoulder and gaze longingly at the past, considering what might have been.

3rd Trap: Pleasure-Seeking

We make the search for happiness our purpose.

Despite what some people may claim, happiness is not a purpose. Happiness is attained as a result of a purpose. For instance, we choose to be a musician. The act of giving something meaningful to the world, of having people tell us that our songs helped them through difficult times, will make us feel valuable and, by extension, happy.

In contrast, if our goal in life exclusively revolves around the search for happiness, this search will, more often than not, deteriorate into a search for pleasure. The reason for this is that, in working solely to please ourselves, we lose the ability to give anything in return. We take and take and take, and while it might satisfy us for a while, we'll soon come to realize that no matter how much we take, it's never enough. Have you ever noticed that an excess of pleasure turns to pain? You enjoy a soothing massage. It feels good for a while, but when overdone, your muscles start to bruise and ache. This type of existence is what leads us down dark and lonely roads like depression and despair.

4th Trap: Running From Reality

We reject reality in favor of escapism.

We spend all of our time on social media, surfing the internet, watching television, playing video games, listening to music, reading books, and so on. If we live this sort of existence, we run the risk of becoming obsessed with living vicariously through others. Granted, such a life might be a lot of fun. But upon reaching a certain age, we'll look back to discover that we've accomplished nothing of our own. Our chance to leave a unique mark on the world has either diminished or completely passed us by.

Motherhood Versus Career:
Sorting Through the Misconceptions

Sofia had done it. She had graduated from university. Her major was political science, her long-term goal to become a corporate attorney. The image of her parents, siblings and cousins sitting in the auditorium, watching her with proud and smiling faces, was a special memory that she brought with her to her new life in Chicago, where she would work to complete her studies at a moderately prestigious law school.

Some days were tougher than others; the reward of a hard day's work was satisfying. Nevertheless, over time, the certainty she'd once had about her career began to weaken. She made an effort to ignore these distractions, but the doubt was powerful enough to disrupt her focus. One thought kept running through her mind: *I don't know if I want to pursue a law degree full-time anymore.* A deep, hidden part of her yearned to marry her boyfriend of three years and have a family. Yet all around her—from the education system to the media, from advertisements to the entertainment industry—society was bombarding her with the message that she couldn't possibly be happy as a mother. "Motherhood is like slavery," one of her teachers claimed. "Children will bring an end to all your personal freedoms," the television warned. "The childfree life is the happiest life," the media insisted.

After enough repetition, the messages took effect.

"Maybe I'm about to make a huge mistake," Sofia told her boyfriend. "Maybe I'm allowing my emotional desire of wanting children to get in the way of the right decision. Maybe I'll regret the decision a few years down the road."

"You won't regret it," Sofia's boyfriend assured. He was calm during arguments, a trait she'd always appreciated. "Millions of people who have children are much happier for it. Plus, you and I both love children. What could possibly make us regret having them?"

Sofia took a few weeks to consider her options, even presenting her dilemma to some female colleagues. Each path came with its own set of pros and cons, but ultimately, the career path seemed to carry less risk. "I don't want to have children," she decided.

Although he was heartbroken and disappointed, Sofia's boyfriend accepted her decision. He ended their relationship soon afterwards, having decided that it was a better use of his time to pursue a girl whose life goals were in line with his own.

Sofia went on to complete law school, pass the bar and become a corporate attorney. While to this day she enjoys her work, she often talks about the past. Now thirty-six, she admits that she wishes she would've, at the very least, chosen to become both a mother and an attorney. Her primary regret was allowing societal norms to influence the biggest decision of her life—not only because the decision wasn't sincere, but because it turned out to be the wrong one.

There is a common misconception, which seems to grow more common every day, that all girls who choose motherhood as their purpose will end up unhappy. Worse, the misconception also claims that all girls who choose motherhood as their purpose are inferior to those who choose a professional career. This couldn't be further from the truth. In itself, motherhood is one of the noblest purposes in the world. Granted, if we are bad mothers who neglect and abuse our children, our purpose loses its nobility. But for all the mothers in the world who love and sacrifice for their children, few purposes can compare.

On the other hand, if we have no desire to ever become

mothers, this doesn't make us bad or wrong. Not in the least. We can be childless while at the same time achieving nobility and effecting meaningful change. The point is that, in recent years, the light our society once shone so brightly upon motherhood has dimmed. These days, mothers live hidden lives, far from the spotlight of acknowledgement. All their pain, all their sacrifices and all their triumphs take place behind the curtain of the world stage. But why? Mothers are responsible for giving birth to and, along with their husbands, raising the new generation: the new inventors, teachers, world leaders, and so on. Not to mention, our mothers are the very reason for our existence. I would not be writing this book right now were it not for my mother; and likewise, none of you would be reading it.

What purpose could possibly be nobler or more necessary?

If your primary dream in life is to have children and be a good mother,never let anyone convince you that your dream is inferior to that of other dreams. Motherhood is a wonderful role and you are a wonderful person for desiring it. If, at any point, you feel undervalued by the world for your choice—which will inevitably happen from time to time due to our society's ever-declining opinion of mothers—take comfort in the millions of other good mothers around you. They know your battle and your struggle, and there will never come a day when they don't understand the value of it.

How To Choose Your Purpose
So It Doesn't Choose You

Even when we know ourselves, choosing our purpose can be difficult if our desired path is demeaned by society. Like Sofia, perhaps we too feel pressured to adopt a certain role. Or perhaps it's not society that's pressuring us. Perhaps we have an overbearing family.

When it comes to the people who are closest to us, their opinions hold greater value than the opinions of society. It can sometimes be helpful to take our loved ones' advice. After all, they generally want what's best for us. They want to see us succeed. They want to know we're in a position to take care of ourselves or to be taken care of.

If we ever find ourselves in a situation where our loved ones are objecting to our chosen purpose, the best course of action is to establish their intent. For example, we're heading down a path that we know is causing harm to us mentally, physically and even spiritually. Our family will likely intervene with a mind to help us, to direct us towards a healthier path. It's times like these when their advice might be worth considering.

If, on the other hand, we want to pursue a neutral goal such as becoming an artist, but our family members don't believe we'll be able to support ourselves through art and are pressuring us to choose a more practical career, the choice should ultimately fall to us. We might have to work extra jobs for awhile, keeping ourselves afloat until we succeed in the art industry, but if becoming an artist is what we truly want, and if it's what we're skilled at, then we should try. The worst life would be one where we're trapped in a career that we never wanted—we only chose it because it was thrust upon us by our loved ones. We might even end up blaming our loved ones for our unhappiness. Our relationships with them will never be the same.

Ultimately, the ways in which we might stumble upon our purpose are countless. Personally, I found my purpose through isolation. During the two years I spent homeschooling, I spent most of my time alone. Once I'd managed to get comfortable in my own mind, I came to find that I enjoyed creativity and started to develop a tendency towards the arts. I painted. I drew. I even sang. But it wasn't until the day I wrote my first poem that I knew I'd found the path I wanted to continue exploring forever.

Depending on the types of girls we are, we might not be able to find our purpose through solitude. Perhaps we'll have to travel the world or attend university. Whatever the solution may be, we have to at least give ourselves a period of focus, away from all distractions. Even if, in the beginning, we find that we lack confidence, we shouldn't allow ourselves to be discouraged. An initial lack of confidence is completely normal. Confidence is nothing more than "being sure of ourselves," meaning that what will ultimately boost our confidence is firstly: choosing our purpose. And secondly: being good at our purpose.

I've received a lot of advice related to choosing my purpose over the course of my life. Naturally, the best advice was always from people much older than I, people whose wisdom was born from decades of experience. While almost all of the advice I've received has been useful, I'll only share the top three.

1st Piece of Advice: Focus on Your Skills

Choose a purpose you're good at.

Without skill, we're at a higher risk of failing to advance in our chosen field. While we can develop skill in most areas if we work hard enough, sometimes it's unrealistic. For example, you want to be a professional swimmer but can't swim. Or you've spent thirty years of your life working as a lawyer and then one day wake up and decide you want to become an astronaut. One in a million people will succeed in accomplishing this, but as a general rule, it lies outside the realm of possibility.

2nd Piece of Advice: Think Solo or Duo

Discern whether your purpose is an individual one or a partnership.

Most of the purposes we end up choosing will be individual

ones, such as becoming a psychiatrist, a nurse or a writer. We don't necessarily need a second person to work with us. We can succeed on our own. But other purposes, such as marriage, are inevitable partnerships. If this is the case, we need to make sure that our partner is on the same page as us. Let's say your primary goal in life is to get married and become a mother. Is it also your boyfriend's primary goal to get married and become a father?

Imagine you've been dating your boyfriend for seven years. You've stuck with him through thick and thin, and even though you are now in your thirties, your boyfriend still hasn't shown any interest in marrying you or having kids. Whenever you bring up the subject, he either directs the conversation somewhere else or outright tells you that his goals are different from your own. In this case, it's probably best to separate, even if you love him. You can't force another person to adopt your dreams. Trying to do so might make the person unhappy and resentful. You will also risk losing the opportunity to bring your own dreams to fruition.

3rd Piece of Advice: Pick One (or More)

Be open to more than one purpose.

Of course, we do need to choose a central purpose, but there's more than enough room for a few smaller purposes (or hobbies) on the side. For example, my main purpose will begin next year when I become a wife—and hopefully soon afterwards, a mother—but as a smaller purpose, I am a writer. Most of us will end up with multiple purposes at some point in our lives, and it might not even be through our own choice. Some of us might be forced to work an extra job to make enough money to care for ourselves or our children.

No matter the purpose you choose, the key is to never feel forced—force breeds regret. There's no better feeling than knowing you've chosen your purpose of your own accord. Then the path ahead is not only clear—it's right. You can charge ahead without inhibitions, without the desire to stop in your tracks, to turn around and to doubtfully question the past.

7

"It is easier to forgive an enemy than to forgive a friend."

—William Blake

When You've Been Betrayed

What's the worst physical injury you've ever experienced? Mine was stepping on a rusty nail while out for a jog. The nail pierced halfway through the sole of my foot. By the time I returned home, dirt and debris were lodged inside the wound and blood was leaking from my shoe. For the next week, I was unable to place pressure on my foot.

In hindsight, I'd take the pain of stepping on a nail a thousand times over the experience of betrayal. Betrayal is the most destructive kind of wound, for more often than not, the hand that dealt it was friendly. While it's true that enemies will likely betray us, the wounds they inflict will never be deep, for we share no bond with them. The people we love on the other hand are people we've allowed into our hearts. We've taken a risk, solely because we love them, and have entrusted them with the most vulnerable parts of ourselves. But all it takes is a single moment of weakness on their part. When this happens, when someone we love breaks our bond of trust, it's one of the most painful experiences we can suffer.

Unfortunately, there is no standard method of overcoming betrayal. No map exists, leading us from point A to point Z, guaranteeing that if we complete all the required steps, we will be rewarded with the "antidote of healing." Furthermore, not all of us will respond to the same antidotes. Our minds are as unique as thumbprints. Methods of healing that help us might prove ineffective for others. Some might heal by receiving emotional support from family and friends; some might heal by seeking counsel from a therapist or a priest; others might heal by focusing their attention outside of themselves, working towards new goals and learning new things.

Similar to dealing with rejection, it's oftentimes necessary to give ourselves time to process the fact that we've been betrayed. Time to be sad, to be weak, to be angry and to rebuild our sense of self-worth. Of course, this doesn't mean we have to grab a megaphone and announce to the whole world that we've been betrayed. To truly heal, we have to do more than acknowledge our pain; we have to face it and accept it. While striving to attain closure is sometimes the most difficult part of betrayal, without it, healing and moving on is impossible.

Throughout my childhood, and even now, I struggled with asking others for emotional support. I had a martyr complex. My pride told me that I didn't need help, that I could overcome every obstacle on my own. In reality, I did need others. We all do.

My pride hindered me from coming to terms with a lot of betrayal over the course of my life, not only because I didn't ask for help, but because I failed to deal with the pain on my own. Instead, I forced the pain into a distant room in my mind and shut the door. For a time, I was fine. Years passed after the fact—I still felt fine. But one day, an event occurred that caused my pain to resurface. The pain hit me hard, bursting to the exterior like an erupting volcano. I broke down. The worst part was that I hadn't realized I was still harboring the pain. I hadn't realized that I still held resentment, that I hadn't been able to forgive. We all have our methods of coping with betrayal, but the bottom line is that this pain must be dealt with. More importantly, we must realize that we are *capable* of overcoming it.

My second boyfriend, Jack, instigated the first real betrayal I experienced. Jack didn't attend my high school, although many of the girls who did attend my high school were competing for his attention. For some reason, he chose to date me—at least publicly—over the other girls.

I was happy, although in hindsight, I can say with certainty that I never loved Jack. I didn't understand what love was back then. I was a naïve teenager who believed she'd grasped the world in its entirety. But the reality was that I knew nothing of human nature. I didn't even know myself. I was only capable of superficial thoughts and infatuation.

Jack and I only dated a few months. My family didn't care for him, to put it lightly. They thought he was a bad influence. They were concerned that he didn't share our religious views and they thought I was too young to be dating. I didn't care. I was too angry to take my family's advice, as I thought they hadn't even given him a chance. I thought the side of him they claimed to have seen was false. I believed only I knew his true side.

A few months later, I traveled to the East Coast to visit my twin sister at her boarding school in New York. I recall the trip being very cathartic for both of us. We hadn't spoken much in the months leading up to my visit, and part of the reason was due to my relationship with Jack.

Upon my return home, one of my friends called me and told me he'd seen Jack kissing another girl at a party over the weekend. Naturally, I was devastated. I distinctly recall having been unable to conceive of betrayal before this moment. I considered betrayal as a shock-tactic designed to make songs and movies more dramatic.

While betrayal is never easy, the first betrayal generally hits us the hardest. And since it's rare that we'll ever come to know the state of mind and motives of the person who betrayed us, we're often doomed to have one-way conversations in our own heads—conversations that can result in us blaming ourselves for the wrongdoings of others. After all, we were the ones who allowed the person to get close to us, which must mean we're a poor judge of character, right?

Wrong. Unless there are reliable signs or even evidence that a person has a tendency towards betrayal—for example, a history of cheating or constantly flirting with other girls in our presence—how could we be expected to know? Yes, we also might be guilty of making mistakes in our relationships. We might have done things to push our boyfriends away. But this is never an excuse for betrayal.

To this day, I'll never understand why I agreed to take Jack back, but I did. It's not the fact that I don't believe those of us who betray can change and become better people, it's the fact that I was aware Jack *hadn't* changed. Two weeks later, my suspicion was confirmed. He betrayed me with a girl at my high school. She wasn't a close friend, more of an acquaintance, but it was worse than the first betrayal because I could now put a face to the person he'd betrayed me with. Even worse, I had to see her every day at school.

It was then I decided enough was enough. Jack wanted to stay together and even promised me he'd change, but I was determined. It took three long months of self-examination, of forcing myself to face the questions of who I truly was, who I wanted to be and whether I was worth anything at all, before I was able to put the past behind me. In a way though, I didn't get over Jack's betrayal until many years later. Not because my wounds needed years to heal, but because I'd failed to confide in anyone, much less acknowledge my own pain. I simply stowed it away and continued on. This was a huge mistake.

Another huge mistake I made in regards to coping with betrayal was that, at various points in my life, I allowed one person's betrayal to destroy my trust in everyone. I stopped giving people the benefit of the doubt and started placing a broad blanket of mistrust over all. I figured that since people were eventually going to betray me, I could avoid their betrayals by never giving them an opportunity to get close to me in the first place. This mentality condemned me to years of surface-level friendships and relationships. I missed out on the depth and sincerity that those who choose to trust are oftentimes rewarded with, and I hugely regret this.

In this particular case, my decision to mistrust was a product of fear rather than pride. Being a political YouTuber, I still grapple with this fear today. Political YouTube is a vast network of commentators, activists and journalists, many of which are in contact behind the scenes—not because we all agree with one another, but because it helps to maintain some kind of solidarity in the face of the internet's ever-increasing censorship. At the very least, most of us speak to one another on occasion. Some of us are even close friends. The problem with political YouTube is that many people are willing to throw each other under the bus to preserve their careers and reputations; to become richer and more famous; to be accepted by the mainstream political scene; and also for simpler reasons like dislike and jealousy.

That said, it will likely come as no surprise that many people in my political network have, at one point or another, betrayed my confidence, spread false rumors about me, and so on. Not just me, but countless others have also either betrayed or been betrayed. What makes trust particularly risky for political YouTubers is the fact that we have the mainstream media relentlessly circling us like a pack of rabid dogs, employing various tactics to glean insider secrets and gossip. More than anything, they want to see us destroyed, to turn us against one another and watch us stomp each other out. This is why, whenever I come across people in our political network who have made the decision not to trust anyone, I understand their reasoning. However, I don't always agree with it.

What is a life without trust? It's a safer life, yes. But it's also a shallower and more disconnected life. Even worse, it's a loveless life, for there can be no love without trust. Choosing to trust, despite the chances of betrayal, will always be the greatest risk, but it will oftentimes also reap the greatest reward.

When You've Been the Betrayer

"Did you start a rumor about Katie Muller?" your mother asks. She's standing in the family room, a cellphone in one hand, an expression of disappointment tightening the smooth lines of her face. "I just got off the phone with Mrs. Muller. Katie's been crying all night."

"It's not a big deal," you insist. "I've had wayworse rumors spread about me."

"You might've been a victim in the past," your mother agrees, "but that doesn't make you a victim regardless of the situation."

You scoff, insulted. You sense your mother is trying to help, but even so, you can't help but feel judged. Almost every single person you've allowed to get close to you has ended up betraying you in some way. Your mother has no idea how deeply and how repeatedly you've been hurt. Not to mention, why should you be nice to others if others aren't nice to you?

"You can't spend your whole life being a victim," your mother continues. "Human nature isn't perfect, which means that everyone, including the best people, are eventually going to let you down…not necessarily in a big way, but at the very least, in small ways. Even if you've suffered betrayals, the injustice you've faced doesn't make it okay for you to switch roles and become the betrayer. I'm really disappointed in you."

You leave the family room, slamming the door behind you.

Your mother's advice is like trying to swallow a spoonful of cod-liver oil. You don't want to accept it. You're tempted to use her example of "human imperfection" as an excuse for your mistake. You might say something along the lines of, "I'm flawed, so you can't expect me to be perfect all the time."

A bad girl isn't someone who lacks perfection, but someone who lacks remorse. If we have no regret for our betrayal and if we have no intention of attempting to make amends, we disqualify ourselves from the decent majority. Those among the decent majority are aware that, when guilty of betrayal, we are oftentimes required to pay a twofold debt.

The first part of the debt relates to responsibility. If we decide to take responsibility for our wrongdoings, we won't be allowed to contrive excuses or blame others. We have to admit to our errors and apologize. Unfortunately, there might be extra, unforeseen prices such as loss that we have to deal with along the way. For example, we betray a friend's trust, and she no longer wants to be our friend as a result. Even if it feels unfair, we have to accept this loss.

The second part of the debt relates to atonement. Atoning for a betrayal is almost never as simple as offering an apology, even if the apology is sincere, and then moving on. We may be required to work for days, months or even years to prove the sincerity of our remorse and our desire to be a better person. If we succeed though, chances are, we'll not only be able to fully heal the betrayal, but rebuild the broken bond of trust.

There is a common phrase, "Once a cheater, always a cheater." In many cases, this might prove true. But it's definitely not true across the board. Even a serial betrayer can change. Like Jack.

A few months ago, I stumbled across an old friend's Instagram. To my surprise, she'd posted a photo of herself and Jack, announcing that they'd recently begun dating. My first instinct was concern. I was sure he'd treat her in the same way that he'd treated me. But once I succeeded in pushing aside my own negative experience with him, I realized how different he looked: healthier, happier, he was even better dressed. Perhaps the fact that he'd had a son a few years back is what spurred his change. In most of his photos, he proudly included his son: the first day of school, sports events, and so on. From what I could see, he loved being a father.

Furthermore, if I know one thing about my friend, it's that she'd never knowingly date a cheater. Most girls wouldn't. And since my friend knew of Jack's past betrayal towards me and still made the decision to date him, it could only be because he's drastically changed for the better.

Believe it or not, the girl at my high school who betrayed me with Jack also changed. While we didn't speak much for a few years following the betrayal, we ended up becoming friends after graduation. She'd found a good job and was in a stable relationship. She and her boyfriend went on to date for nearly ten years before he proposed; they're planning to get married sometime next year. The point is that some people simply go through bad periods, but these bad periods aren't destined to define them for their entire lives.

In contrast, I know of another serial cheater who, even after being given several chances to change, was unable to do so...

Damien was a husband and a father to three children. But despite this, despite having a wonderful wife and family at home, he repeatedly cheated and even ended up impregnating one of his mistresses. Damien's wife separated from him upon learning he was having a baby with another woman, but several years later, agreed to give him another chance. For awhile, her decision seemed like it had been the right one. But then, after walking the straight and narrow for about two years, Damien stumbled back into his old ways. He cheated. This time, his wife separated from him permanently.

It's always a noble virtue to be forgiving and to be open to offering second, third and even fourth chances as Damien's wife did. Unfortunately, one-sided efforts aren't enough. All successful relationships require a combined effort of two individuals.

8

"We gather our arms full of guilt as though it were precious
stuff. It must be that we want it that way."

— John Steinbeck

When Guilt is a Blindfold

"Please make your way to your assigned seats. Testing will begin in
five minutes."

The classroom lights were brightening as Nora found her seat
in the middle row. Students streamed anxiously to their assigned
positions, filling eight levels of horseshoe-shaped bleachers. Nora
shrugged off her blazer, her hands trembling fitfully, and loosened
the collar of her button-down shirt. The head pains had started an
hour ago; she hadn't taken Adderall that morning. Her stash had
run dry. She'd planned to pick up another bottle before exams
started, but her supplier had jacked his prices due to decreased

competition on campus—and during exam time, no less. She wasn't the only one who was outraged.

Weeks she'd spent studying for these tests. Scoring poorly wasn't an option, not if she intended to graduate with Honors. But without the Adderall...

Still shaking, she sipped from a water bottle she kept tucked in her bag.

"Hey, you feeling okay?" someone whispered.

"Just nervous," Nora replied.

"Yeah, totally."

The Professor rose from his desk at the front of the room. "You may begin," he said, scanning the bleachers through square, silver-rim glasses.

Nora inhaled a thin breath, now nauseated. With a trembling hand, she picked up her pencil, opened her test booklet and read the first essay question.

Those of us who are perfectionists will know that guilt is not always positive. At times, it can feel like more of a curse than a blessing. We're incapable of putting anything out into the world that isn't flawless. Not only this, but we brutalize ourselves whenever we fall short—in our personal and professional lives, and if we're religious, in our spiritual lives.I know a girl who mentally beat herself up every time she forgot to say her morning prayers. We have to cut ourselves some slack on occasion. Granted, the need for perfection might seem noble on the surface; the problem is, it's unrealistic. A perfectionist complex pushes us to extreme lengths to achieve a goal, which can result in the deterioration of our physical and mental health. The fact is: we're never going to achieve perfection, least of all in our own eyes.

My twin sister, Nicole, and I have struggled with perfectionism for most of our lives. We used to delete entire chapters of our science-fiction book shortly after writing them because we were unsatisfied with some aspect or another. In fact, we rewrote our book from white paper over fifteen times, and even then, we weren't content. The only way we were finally able to press "publish" was when we came to terms with our limitations.

Whether we realize it or not, there's a world of difference between aspiring to perfection and demanding it. Aspiring to perfection is noble and moral, but demanding it isn't because human nature is inherently flawed. Moreover, demanding perfection from ourselves or others will cause unhappiness and discontent in our lives because, sooner or later, we're always going to let ourselves or others down. Our lives will never be as perfect as an Instagram post with a filter. Others might be under the delusion that we're perfect or that our creations are perfect, but if we are honest with ourselves, we'll never share this delusion. We know the truth.

And the truth is okay. There's no failure in trying our best, even if our best turns out to be lacking on occasion. We can always work harder, return to the starting line and try again.

When Guilt is a Guiding Light

"Why did you do it?" your friend asks you.

A weight, like rocks, builds up in your stomach. You bite your tongue, knowing that if you try to speak, you'll cry. Every time you move, it's as if the edges of the rocks are cutting you from the inside. You just want to disappear.

Most of us have experienced a similar guilty feeling. Generally, guilt comes to us in the form of pain, but this particular pain isn't one related to sickness. Like an ever-present ally, guilt swoops in to separate our good deeds from our bad; it proves that we still know right from wrong.

The fact that this pain is healthy doesn't automatically make it easy to live with. Oftentimes, it's unbearable, torturing us from the moment we wake to the moment we sleep. Perhaps this is because, more often than not, we feel powerless to switch off our own guilt. We feel that the only thing capable of easing it is forgiveness from the person we hurt.

What do we do, then, when the person we hurt tells us they will never forgive us? Our remorse is sincere, and we even work hard to make amends, but still their heart remains closed. "You're dead to me," they say. In this case, we might feel our pain is incurable.

I once had a political friend, Violet. We used to spend hours talking over the phone, discussing our various interests and political concerns, and even confiding in one another. Violet was gorgeous, with loose brown curls and a husky laugh that sounded sleepy; unfortunately, I never got the chance to meet her in person. One day, Violet called me with a request. She wanted me to make a YouTube video that would raise awareness on a certain political issue. While I agreed with the issue in question, I thought the photos she wanted me to use were too extreme. The political issue was controversial in and of itself; adding the photos would only fan the flames, and possibly cause YouTube to ban me. I admit I was too afraid to take the risk. I told her no.

Violet ended the call. Without another word, she took to social media, calling me a "coward" and a "wolf in sheep's clothing." She wrote that I'd let her down as a friend and that it was impossible to meet reliable people anymore. While I'd expected Violet to be angry, her level of anger took me completely by surprise. The way she spun the situation made me sound like some kind of monster. However, as I read her Facebook posts, I do recall questioning if I'd made the right decision—if there was some truth to her words. She was right in the sense that my reaction had been in part due to fear.

I apologized to Violet, but she refused to forgive me. To this day, she still hasn't spoken to me.

Obviously, this example of guilt isn't severe. Many of us, myself included, have made far worse mistakes which we've sought forgiveness for. We might have lied, stolen, cheated or even ruined someone's reputation. If we're denied forgiveness, though, the worst thing we can do as a means to cope is to drive out our guilt.

Three summers ago, an old friend called me out of the blue over Skype. I remember thinking it strange that she was calling, for we hadn't spoken so much as a word to each other in over a year.

"Wow, Molly, it's been a long—" I cut off as Molly appeared. Pale and emaciated, she looked as if she hadn't slept in days. Her swollen, red face glistened haggardly through the Skype screen and her expression wore a far-away look.

"Sorry if I'm bothering you," she said softly. "I just need someone to talk to."

"You're not bothering me at all, Molly," I assured. "We can talk as long as you want."

"I just—" She clenched her teeth, clearly suppressing tears. "I just want to give up."

At first, I wasn't sure how to respond. I've never been great at comforting others. Plus, Molly's drastically changed appearance still hadn't registered. Although still pretty, she'd lost the spark she'd had before moving to New York City to pursue a modeling career.

"Did…something bad happen with your modeling?" I asked.

She laughed, an abrupt and hollow sound. "More than one bad thing…"

"But you always look so happy in all your social media posts," I said. And it was true; in every photo, Molly was smiling—with friends at lavish parties, with fellow models at fashion events, with her boyfriend on romantic dates. It seemed like she'd been living the high life.

"I'm successful now, yeah, but not happy," Molly said. "When I first moved to New York, I couldn't book a job. It was hard to make friends. I did meet a guy, though…we ended up dating for eight months." She swallowed hard, each word an effort. "Noah was a good guy, just not a good boyfriend. He was…neglectful."

I felt like I knew where the story was headed, but I didn't interrupt.

"A year ago, I booked my first job," Molly continued. "I was happy because the job got me attention from other agencies. From there, I was booking jobs regularly. The craziest part was that people started to notice me: I got invited to parties. A few celebrities asked me out and others sent me gifts. I even gained fifteen-thousand followers on social media." She paused to rub her eyes, which were now red and swollen. "I don't know how to describe it other than my life changed overnight. It was as if, suddenly one day everyone realized I was special…except for Noah." She shook her head. "He didn't even seem to care. He was always busy with his own job. Sometimes, two weeks would pass without so much as a text message. At this point, I'd break down and call him up, telling him that I needed him."

"Did you cheat on him?" I asked quietly.

A tear rolled down Molly's cheek. She wiped it away and sat in silence a while. Finally, she nodded. "Yeah...with a guy I hardly knew. I felt so bad that I broke up with Noah the next day. It was like I'd unleashed something dark inside myself. I knew what I was doing was wrong, but somehow, I managed to block out the guilt. For the next couple of months, I jumped from party to party and from guy to guy. I even...started doing drugs."

Molly was sobbing now. The urge to comfort her arose, but I resisted. I knew that a desire for validation wasn't why she'd called. Had validation been her motive, I probably would've hung up a long time ago.

"What woke you up?" I asked.

"Visiting home a few weeks ago." She sniffled. "Being back with my family, seeing all my old friends and going back to church made me realize that modeling isn't the life I want. I'm not this person, Britt. I want to leave New York. I want to go home, and I want to meet a nice guy...maybe even start a family. The problem is—"

Molly didn't have to say another word. I could already see that she didn't believe she deserved a second chance.

"Did you ever tell Noah that you cheated?" I asked.

"I wanted to," Molly said. "But by the time I woke up, we'd been broken up for months. I didn't even know where he was anymore. When I visited home, I asked a priest for advice. He told me it wasn't necessary to contact Noah because he was no longer in my life. Instead, he told me that I needed to make amends in other ways."

"Why don't you?"

Molly gripped her head in her hands, sobbing loudly. "Because I can't, Britt. I've gone too far. I used to be the girl who looked down on other girls for cheating on their boyfriends, and now...now I'm one of them." She wiped her nose on her shirt sleeve. "But it's not me, Britt, I promise. I just got lost for a while. I'd never do something like this again."

I believed Molly, but I didn't tell her so. Instead, I listened in silence until she stopped talking. My first instinct was to wait and see what Molly did next. Molly knew as well as I did that apologies, even sincere apologies, weren't enough.

Eventually, Molly did show remorse through her actions. A few weeks later, she left New York. She moved back home with her family, reconnected with her old friends and started going back to church. Ultimately, given the choice between fame and anonymity, she chose the latter. To this day, Molly hasn't dated anyone. I assume it's because she's taking time to "work on herself," because these were the last words she spoke to me.

No one, not even the greatest sinner, is irredeemable—at least not in the eyes of God. Plus, sometimes good people make mistakes because they're simply in a bad state-of-mind. They allow themselves to go too far, but right before hitting rock bottom, they catch themselves. Perhaps, in Molly's case, she wouldn't have gone so far if she hadn't tried to suppress her guilt.

In a way, shutting off our guilt is like shutting off our moral compass. Without a guiding light, the path ahead becomes blurred. It's a bit like existing on autopilot. Mistake after mistake after mistake…until, like Molly, we no longer recognize ourselves.

The main revelation I had during my conversation with Molly was that, even if we're forgiven by others, it's almost always insufficient. While receiving forgiveness from others is extremely important—and oftentimes necessary for certain people to move on—what's even more necessary is forgiving ourselves. Forgiveness from others might give us the stability-of-mind to forge ahead in the short-term, but forgiveness of self is what gives us the stability-of-mind to forge ahead in the long-term.

9

"To err is human; to forgive, divine."

—Alexander Pope

Mercy Looking Upon Misery

I don't usually share inspirational quotes on social media, although I do like to collect them privately; I've accumulated hundreds in folders on my computer. One such quote, told to me by a priest five years ago, concerns forgiveness. He described forgiveness as "mercy looking upon misery." This description left a deep impression on me. It made me view the act of forgiving in an entirely new light.

During my early teens, I was a lot more hardheaded towards the concept of forgiveness than I am now, particularly when it came to forgiving bigmistakes. I figured that if a person messed up in a big way, it was proof that they didn't truly care about me.

What ultimately changed my mind was finding myself in a situation where I was the person who needed to be forgiven.

In high school, I was close friends with a girl named Megan. She and her boyfriend, Kristian, dated for about three years before breaking up. A month or so after their breakup, Kristian and I went on a few dates. The dates were nothing serious; we were just getting to know one another. But things took a downward turn when I discovered that news of our dates had upset Megan. Apparently, she still hadn't gotten over him.

Right away, I broke off the relationship. I felt guilty about the situation. I was sure that my friendship with Megan would change because of my insensitivity. I realized I'd been selfish not to mention dating Kristian to her beforehand, especially because we were close friends. Had our roles been reversed, I would've been upset too.

The next day after school, I pulled Megan aside and apologized. "I'm sorry if I hurt you," I said. "I won't go out with Kristian again."

The awkward moments of silence that passed still remain distinct in my memory. Each moment grew heavier, tormenting me with the prospect of rejection.

"It's okay," Megan finally said. "I'm not mad at you and it means a lot—you coming to talk. It's hard right now, seeing him date other girls, but I guess that's normal. I won't be upset if you want to go out with him again. I get that we both need to move on."

Megan then said she had to leave, but before doing so, hugged me. I'll never forget the relief that washed over me as she did so. Whether she realized it or not, Megan gave me the biggest gift she could have possibly given me that day. Because after that experience, I knew what it felt like to have to ask for mercy. I never wanted anyone, not even my worst enemy, to have to feel such pain on my account.

Some people believe it's impossible for love and hurt to coexist. In my opinion, these people are overly idealistic. While I certainly don't believe that love is always destined to share a bed with severe wounds, there will always be smaller wounds, like forgetting to call or mixing up the date of a loved one's birthday.

Whether the wound is small or large, most of us understand that forgiveness is a necessary part of life. We're humble enough to acknowledge human imperfection, while at the same time strong enough to accept it. But not everyone shares this point of view.

Imagine there are two very different girls: Mary is mild-tempered and cheerful. She is so timid that she stands against the wall during parties, then before the night ends, heads for the nearest exit without speaking a word. Evelyn, with her dark hair and fiery temper, lets no one push her around. The one thing these two girls share in common is that their reputations have been ruined by the same internet rumor.

The girl responsible for starting the internet rumor did so out of jealousy. But after watching the storm she created unravel on social media, remorse overwhelms her. She visits Mary and Evelyn at their homes, asking for forgiveness.

"I've put out a video, telling everyone the rumor's false," she says. "I'm so sorry. I'll do anything I can to fix it."

Mary does not want to forgive the girl. She's cried every night since the incident, for the initial bad rumor has escalated into cyberbullying from hundreds of anonymous internet users. There's no putting the rumor back in the bottle, no chance of convincing the entire internet of its falsity—the rumor has already gone viral. Her reputation will never be the same. Mary wants to shout at the girl. She wants her to feel the same pain she's felt. But instead, forcing all of the hurt aside, she says, "It's okay. I forgive you."

Evelyn feels the exact same anger towards the perpetrator. An apology isn't enough, not even close. When the girl comes to ask forgiveness, all the pain and rage Evelyn's been feeling comes to the surface. "You can't fix it, you dumb bitch," she says. "You've already ruined me. I can't believe you'd even come here and ask."

Some of us may think that Evelyn is justified in denying forgiveness. But in a way, since all humans are imperfect, refusing to forgive is no different than saying "others should have to suffer for their faults, but I shouldn't have to suffer for mine." Like Evelyn, those of us who are unable to forgive might seem strong and confident on the surface, but what none of us can claim is that Evelyn has more strength than Mary. Evelyn's weakness becomes obvious the moment a girl like Mary comes along.

However, forgiving someone in no way means that our relationship with them has to return to normal—to how life was before the person made the mistake. In fact, if we so choose, we never have to speak to the person again. Depending on how big the mistake was, we're completely justified in cutting them out of our lives. Despite what some people may believe, forgiveness isn't the same as absolving a person of the need to take responsibility for their mistakes and to make amends.

The reason forgiveness is so important is that it can do much to motivate a person to be better. In giving others a second chance, we're giving them an opportunity to learn from their mistakes and to make the right choice the next time around. If we deny them forgiveness, however, it might cause them to believe they're irredeemable. They might even give up, riding the downward spiral all the way to the bottom.

As a whole, I think we can all agree that the world today is not a forgiving place. We are punished for mistakes that we made decades ago, and sometimes we're even punished for mistakes that we didn't personally make, but that someone we're associated with made. Most of us no longer want to forgive, we only want to judge. The last thing on our minds is turning our judgements inwards and examining ourselves. Perhaps we're too afraid of the darkness that we'll find.

But the truth is, in a world of imperfection, forgiveness is always going to be necessary. If others are too weak to forgive us, despite us being sincerely sorry, we have no choice but to make peace with the fact that we tried our best. Our remorse, our will to make amends, and our desire to be better puts us in the right. No matter how bad the mistake we've made is, few deeds are so bad that they can't eventually be paved over with good ones.

10

"You must remember to love people and use things, rather than to love things and use people."
—Fulton J. Sheen

Self-Worth on Steroids

The volleyball court echoed with shuffling feet. Behind me, a teammate intercepted a hit from the opposing team and passed the ball to the setter. The setter teased the ball gracefully into the air using the tips of her fingers and shouted, "Five."

My number. "Five" meant she was positioning the ball to the left side of the net. I angled towards the ball, swinging in for a quick approach, cocking my arm in preparation for a hit—when suddenly, a second body appeared at my side.

"I've got it," Lana grunted. She pushed me out of the way and spiked the ball into a well-aimed corner, scoring a point for the team.

My teammates came in for a group high-five, everyone except for Lana. She remained up at the net, her eyes bright at the roaring applause.

"Stop being a ball hog," I muttered to Lana, as I returned to my spot on the court.

"It's not ball hogging," Lana said coolly. "It's called being a better player than you."

My hands clenched at my sides. I itched to fire back, but in the end, decided that starting drama in the middle of a game wasn't worth it. Our coach was all about discipline, and I didn't feel like running makeup laps after the game.

As the game wore on, Lana continued hogging the ball. Worse, she screamed at our setter every time she failed to set her up with a perfect hit. Screwing up during a game was never Lana's fault; it was always the fault of another player. Soon, most of the teammates were complaining about Lana under their breath.

"Let's give her to the other team as a trophy if they win," one girl suggested.

"Why won't coach just sub her out?" another complained.

The game wound down. Lana again stole the ball from another girl and scored the winning point. The crowd leapt to their feet, cheering. As I joined the team huddle on the edge of the court, collapsing into a chair, my frustration reached a tipping point.

The cheering crowd swarmed Lana, who was now thoroughly

smiling. She pumped her fists in the air as they lifted her on their shoulders, content to accept all the glory and disregarding those who had helped her to achieve it.

In my author's note, I mentioned that one of the main issues girls struggle with is too little self-worth. However, some girls, like Lana, struggle with the opposite: too much self-worth. Girls who make themselves the center of the universe not only dote on themselves in excessive ways, but they expect others to do the same. Unfortunately, in the same way that we can't love others when we lack self-worth, we also can't love others when we have too much. Our focus is constantly drawn inward, our minds constantly absorbed in admiring our own talents and in satisfying our own desires. Of course, this type of girl has no time to consider others.

Nowadays, a lot of celebrities appear to have big egos. This impression might be accurate in some cases, although in my opinion it probably isn't one-hundred percent honest for the most part. More likely than not, it's a persona the celebrity has adopted in order to make themselves more famous. If they were really so conceited, no one would like them or want to be around them, at least not for friendly reasons.

Certain professions seem to be a magnet for self-important people: modeling, sports, acting, singing, YouTubing, and of course, politics. Looking closely, we find that the underlying factor in these different professions is the same: money and fame.

Let's say that you've managed to attract half a million Twitter
followers. A few of your followers send you hate every now and
again, but for the most part, you're showered with compliments.
Day in and day out, your followers tell you how great you are, how
beautiful, intelligent, sexy, talented and humorous. At first, the
compliments bounce off because underneath the glamour, you
know your own flaws. But one day, after achieving a particularly
huge goal, you're in a good mood and you allow yourself to
entertain the possibility that your followers might be right. Their
compliments start to sink in, distorting your vision of yourself and
reconstructing your reality. Soon, you are convinced that you're
superior to others.

There are more than a few self-important people in my
political network. These people are so accustomed to being
admired that they get upset when they attend an event where one
of their fellow political activists receives more attention than they
do. Since they're in the habit of receiving daily attention from their
fan-bases, they can't conceive of being overlooked. They don't
know how to process anonymity.

What's more, they begin to view the world through an artificial
lens. They, along with other famous and wealthy people, appear to
themselves to be standing on a higher level than their fans. Of
course, this is a skewed perception. No person, not even the most
famous person in the world, is of inherently greater value than
anyone else. Granted, our roles in life might have unequal value.

For instance, our sacrifices might never equal the sacrifice of a soldier who gives his life for his country. Or we may not bear as much responsibility as others, like the leader of a country, and in this way, we might deserve less admiration. But where we are equal is in our souls.

On the other hand, we can't be too hard on self-important people. Perhaps they haven't decided that they're better than others of their own volition. Their lofty perception of themselves might have been built up solely by admirers and fans. This is why, in many cases, whenever their followings lag or even drop, so does their self-esteem. Some go to extreme lengths to regain their popularity—sometimes with crazy videos, attention-seeking scandals, or even dangerous stunts. Pride and vanity have the potential to poison even the best of us, particularly if we don't have people in our lives who are willing to pull us back down to earth.

Self-obsession hasn't posed much of an issue for me throughout the course of my life. In truth, I suffer more from the opposite. But I would be lying if I didn't admit I was sometimes tempted to grow a big head. If we ever find ourselves in a position where we're repeatedly showered with praise, we should take a second to remember that we're not perfect. The positive opinions of others can most certainly be true, but this is not always the case. Such a mentality can also prove helpful when we're on the receiving end of negative opinions, for we'll be able to identify them as subjective and brush them off more easily.

Fortunately, God blessed me with a good family—good parents, brothers and sisters who are willing to lovingly pull me back down to earth whenever I get a little too big-headed. Although some people might regard this type of honesty as harsh, I regard it as necessary. My family knows what's best for me. They're aware that, without humility, all my accomplishments would lose their nobility. They understand that if every now and again I don't have a hand helping to keep me on the straight and narrow, I'll inevitably stray off the path.

How many of us know a person who thinks so little of us and so much of themselves that they take the time to contact us only when they need something? The majority of us likely know at least one person; it's the kind of person we never hear from, sometimes for months at a time, but then one day out of the blue, they descend back into our lives with some new request. Granted, there's nothing wrong with asking for favors in general, but if the person asking is never willing to give anything in return, only the saints among us will want to oblige.

If we aren't willing to offer ourselves for the benefit of others, if we're only willing to use others for our own benefit, our very existence becomes parasitical. Unfortunately, becoming a user is the most common symptom of self-obsession. Since we're incapable of loving others, our only option is to exploit them as a means to our own selfish end. Slowly but surely, people morph from human beings into instruments, like chess pieces in a game.

While certain people might pretend to like us, their love will never be authentic. The reason for this is that, ultimately, we attract the type of people that we are. If we're users, we'll also attract users—who will abandon us the moment our beauty, talent, money or fame runs dry. We'll end up unloved and alone.

11

"Everything in moderation, including moderation."
—Oscar Wilde

It's All About Balance

Have you ever been so consumed with work or with personal projects that you didn't even allow yourself a break to celebrate your own birthday? I have. I've missed out on celebrating birthdays, holidays, and even family vacations.

Six years ago, my father planned a family vacation to Montana. Yellowstone Park is one of his favorite places in the world. Weeks he spent organizing horseback rides, hikes, water-rafting, camping. For weeks he excitedly anticipated having the family all together again. Everyone in my family, myself included, agreed to go.

But as the date of the vacation drew near, I started to panic. I still needed a few more weeks to finish the draft of the book I was working on. Fearing that going on a vacation would interrupt my flow or even cause me to lose motivation, I pulled my mother aside two days before the vacation and told her I couldn't go.

"What?" my mother asked. A look of surprise eclipsed her usual pleasant expression. "But this trip means so much to your dad. You have to go."

"I know, and I want to go. But I have to work," I insisted. "If I don't finish writing this draft within the next three weeks, I won't be able to query agents in the fall."

My mother sighed. "It's your choice. I won't force you to go. But your dad's going to be disappointed—not only him, but your brothers and sisters as well."

I knew she was right. Most of my seven siblings weren't living at home at this time, so I rarely saw them; it would be at least another year before we'd have another family get-together. Even so, my obsession with work won out. Looking back, I hugely regret my choice. I don't remember the happiness of writing those pages, but I would've remembered the happiness of making memories with my family. I would've had the opportunity to strengthen my relationships with them, and even more importantly, I wouldn't have hurt my father.

What I hadn't yet learned is that moderation is the key to a stable life. I didn't understand the need for delegating specific time to work, to family, to entertainment, to religion and to myself. I also didn't understand that being too obsessive or too extreme always comes with a price. Whether that price is a deterioration of personal relationships or experiencing a mental and physical burnout, the question isn't *if* it will come, it's *when*.

I've experienced two burnouts at two different points during my time as a political activist. The burnouts were largely due to the fact that I didn't know where to draw the line. I agreed to take on every project that caught my interest. I answered "yes" to every favor that others asked of me. Soon, I was in over my head, buried under a workload that made it nearly impossible for me to celebrate Christmas with my family last year. Trips to London, Budapest, Dresden, Halle, and Frankfurt to cover political events and demonstrations. Weekly videos, including dozens of interviews and even an in-depth video series.

The work never ended. I had little time to eat and sleep. Nights I spent in a dazed stupor, trying to be productive. The quality of my work suffered. So did my mental and physical health. Thankfully, my mother, my twin sister and fiancé took note of my state and intervened, convincing me to take a breather and lay low for a few months.

Of course, moderation applies to more than our jobs. It applies to all areas of our lives, including our personal relationships. For example, let's say you meet a young man you're interested in. He asks you on a date, and almost immediately, you form a special connection. This connection becomes attachment, which eventually devolves into obsession. You find yourself dedicating every waking moment to either spending time with him, doing him favors, planning romantic gestures or thinking about him. As a result, you ignore your family and friends. You also ignore the fact that it's impossible to maintain a long-term relationship at such a rate. After a few months, you wake up and find yourself exhausted. You assume that the reason for your exhaustion is because relationships are demanding, when in reality, you're not actually in a *normal* relationship. Or you might think you're exhausted because you've contributed more than your boyfriend in the relationship, when in reality, you're far too extreme for any normal male to match. Ultimately, your fatigue will detract from your interest in your boyfriend. You might even decide to end the relationship, just to get a break.

No matter the area of our lives, if we hope to achieve long-term success, the answer is almost always through moderation. Moderation is the key to finding a balance between lack of self-worth and too much self-worth. The most successful people in the world have at some point worked to establish moderation in their lives—a specific routine that they follow and rarely break. They know the inestimable value of a balanced body and mind.

On the other hand, the fact that so many of us struggle with achieving moderation nowadays isn't exactly surprising. Our society is drawn to extremes, and more often than not, fuels the fire of our struggle.

When was the last time you saw an advertisement that said: *Love yourself in a stable and healthy way.*

Never.

Instead, we see advertisements that say: *Love yourself because you're the greatest and most perfect person to ever grace the planet with her presence.*

The message is never to find one man to love forever; it's to have sex with dozens of them until our bodies feel used, until our minds lose their hopefulness and vitality, until our hearts are weary. The message is never to work towards a healthy body weight; it's to either starve ourselves until we're extremely thin, or eat until we're obesely fat because all sizes are "beautiful." The message is never to sacrifice for the ones we love; it's to have a divorce lawyer on speed dial in preparation for the moment when our personal comfort and happiness suffers. The message is never to implement sensible border security for our country; it's to fling the doors open wide and let the entire world in. Our society has gone so far past the point of moderation that it's hinging on hysteria.

When we're constantly being bombarded with such messages, it's no wonder that achieving moderation is difficult. But despite this—despite the ever-increasing hysteria—if we manage to achieve moderation, our lives will be infinitely happier, more effective and sustainable.

12

"There is nothing noble in being superior to your fellow man;
true nobility is being superior to your former self."
—Ernest Hemingway

Attracting the Good with Your Goodness
(Including a Good Man)

At one point during my teenage years, I decided not to date until
after I'd published a book. I held this mindset, even after
acknowledging that publishing a book might take five-to-ten
years. Admittedly, this decision was extreme, but as the previous
chapter made clear, I struggle with finding and maintaining a
balance.

Three long years passed. I spent the days buried in work,
disregarding parties and most social events in general. At times,
particularly when I came across happy couples, I felt lonely. Rather

than acknowledge my need for social comfort, I ran from my feelings. *I can't afford to date,* I told myself. *A boyfriend would be a distraction.*

By the end of the third year, my loneliness had become more than a discomfort; it had become the cause of periodic sadness in my life. My achievements weren't enough to satisfy me. I continued to feel a deep longing for something more. Social interaction wasn't as easy to turn down at this point. I found myself constantly thinking about how nice it would be to meet someone who I could care for and share my life with. After some consideration, I chose to reverse my previous decision and open the "dating door."

For the next few months, I attended various parties, social events and community gatherings, hoping to meet a nice young man. No luck. Feeling a bit discouraged, I thought to myself, *Where have all the good men gone?*

The question stuck with me. I figured the reason I couldn't meet a nice young man concerned the selection I had, rather than a problem with myself.

One morning, while having a coffee in the kitchen with my mother, I posed her the same question.

"Where are all the good guys, mom? They seem to have been a lot better back when you were young."

My mother smiled, an unmistakable glint of humor in her expression; clearly, she thought I'd asked her a stupid question.

"The good guys...well," she began. "Have you ever considered the possibility that there's a reason they aren't interested in you?"

I blinked at her in silence for a moment, insulted. I hadn't expected this reply.

"Good qualities attract good qualities," my mother went on. "If you're a good woman, you'll find a good man."

I searched for a way to argue back, but couldn't think of an excuse. There was too much truth in her words. In reality, I was in no place to demand a boyfriend who was loving, honorable and loyal. I was still far too immature and selfish, and I also worked too much. I recall leaving the kitchen being unable to put her words out of my mind. To this day, I'm still unable to put them out of my mind, particularly because they don't apply only to boyfriends, but to every person in our lives. As good girls, we'll attract good friends and perhaps even influence our struggling friends to become better. As for our children, they will be far more likely to adopt good qualities if they're exposed to our virtues on a daily basis.

Perhaps what makes it difficult for many of us to arrive at such conclusions of our own volition is because, again, our society constantly tells us the opposite. The world today has a false conception of worthiness. Irresponsible people get famous. Decadent people are placed on a pedestal. Shallow people acquire large social media followings. Greedy people attain wealth and prestige. Corrupt people attain power. Status and acceptance are no longer gained by personal merit, but handed out based on personal belief.

This is not worthiness; in fact, it's an inversion of the term. While I've come to learn what true worthiness is, the people who taught me never did so in words. My father showed me worthiness when he spent forty years working jobs he disliked to support my siblings and me. My mother showed me worthiness when she walked away from an elite education and dedicated her life to caring for my siblings and me. My twin, Nicole, showed me worthiness when she refused to abandon me, even during the times I deserved it. My sister showed me worthiness when she suffered through months of agonizing surgeries in order to give birth to her son. My sister's husband showed me worthiness when he took care of my sister, even feeding and bathing her during her months of recovery. My friend, Juliette, showed me worthiness when she helped me to overcome my biggest fault, not through shame and judgement but through tenderness and compassion. My friend, Lauren, showed me worthiness when she traveled to some of the most dangerous locations in the world, risking her life to film and expose the truth. My friend, Melissa, showed me worthiness when she forgave me for letting her down during the darkest period of my political activism. My fiancé, Martin, showed me worthiness when he risked his career, reputation and oftentimes his life to stand up for what was right; when he faced each new hardship with a smile, persevering through violent attacks, legal trials, slander and financial oppression; when he showed me that no matter how bad things got, he would never give up, and even more importantly, that he would never surrender his honor.

For the past twenty-six years, these people have shownme what worthiness is: that it's measured not in how much we choose to do for ourselves, but in how much we choose to do for others. While I may fall short on occasion, I take comfort in the fact that I have people in my life who will never cast me aside; they will always be there to lift me up, to help me find the will to persevere and overcome.

Perhaps not all of us are fortunate to have such good people in our lives, but we canattract them. In working to become the best versions of ourselves, good people, including a good young man, will be drawn to us—people who will stand by us, even at our lowest points, guiding us back to the straight and narrow.

13

"Daringly dared, half of it won."
—Swedish Proverb

Dear Girls...

With the courage to try at least once and the perseverance to try at least twice, we've already conquered half our pursuit. We're also already ahead of the crowd, for the majority of the crowd never reaches the point of taking the first step.

I can't fail if I don't try, is the mentality.

The truth is that those of us who are most unlikely to fail are those of us who try. Because failure is much more than making a mistake—it's a loss of hope. We can fall a thousand times, but unless we decide otherwise, the possibility remains of getting back up. Yes, there will be hardships. Tomorrow, the next day, and the next day after that. But we're never alone. Every girl in the world, myself included, faces a battle for worthiness. If we're able to conquer this battle (through trying, trying, and trying again), nothing will be able to stop us from reaching the day when we're capable of loving ourselves, loving others, and even showing others how to love.

As I mentioned in the beginning of this book, I used to believe that I was incapable of befriending girls, but thankfully, I managed to overcome this flaw. I came to realize that female solidarity isn't only a practical pursuit, but a critical one. Of course, when I use the term "female solidarity," I'm not referring to the kind of female solidarity where we refuse to take responsibility for our own life choices and actions, and come together as self-perceived victims; I'm referring to the kind of female solidarity where we come together as confidants and advisors, helping one another to overcome our faults in order to become the best girls that we can be. Perhaps some of you have already found such girlfriends; if so, you're more blessed than you might realize. For those of you who haven't, however, I encourage you to seek them out. Who knows, the next girl you meet might end up being the most steadfast and reliable friend of your life...and you might end up being hers.

Good luck, and Sincerely,

Brittany Pettibone

CPSIA information can be obtained
at www.ICGtesting.com
Printed in the USA
FSHW021400291218
54748FS